SALONE
barbiere
MP

U.S. ARMY RANGERS & SPECIAL FORCES
OF WORLD WAR II

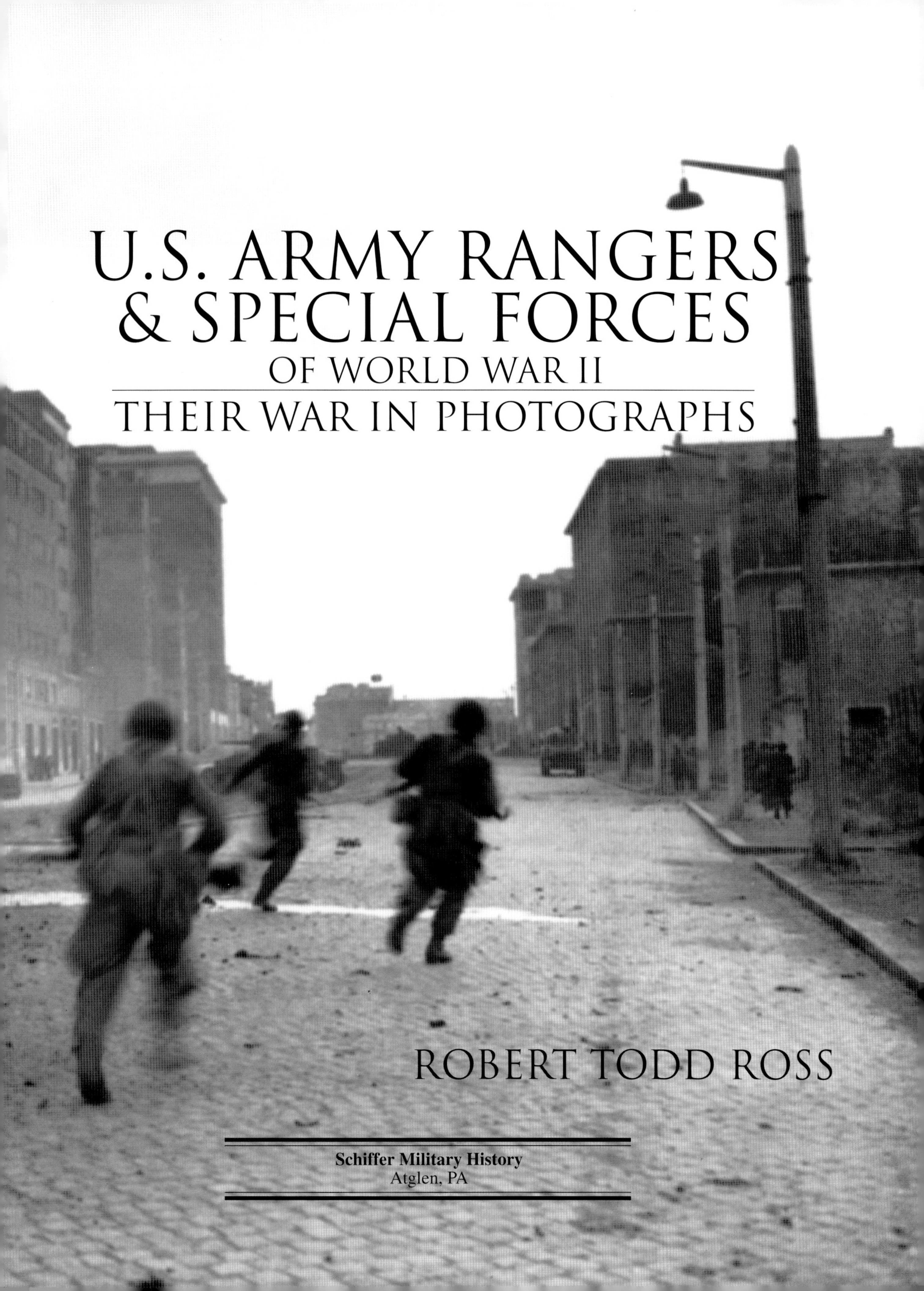

U.S. ARMY RANGERS & SPECIAL FORCES OF WORLD WAR II

THEIR WAR IN PHOTOGRAPHS

ROBERT TODD ROSS

Schiffer Military History
Atglen, PA

Acknowledgments

The author wishes to thank the following people whose valuable assistance contributed to the completion of this book: Pete Bennethum, Ken Bennett, Peter J. Bonner, Mills C. Brandes (2671st Special Reconnaissance Battalion, OSS), Hal Braun (158th Infantry Regiment, Separate), Dr. Mort Cohen, August C. Erdbrink (First Special Service Force), Kenneth E. Gummel (1st & 3rd Ranger Battalions), Elizabeth Heasman, Carl H. Lehmann (1st & 3rd Ranger Battalions), Leonard G. Lomell (2nd Ranger Battalion), Mike Marine, Teresa Moreno, Hayes Otoupalik, Joe Ranoia, Kirk B. Ross, Virginia Schry, J. Robert Slaughter (29th Ranger Battalion, Provisional), Edward Trey (83rd Chemical Mortar Battalion), Morten Tuftedahl (99th Infantry Battalion, Separate), Richard Whelan, Lance Q. Zedric, and the National Archives & Records Administration Still Pictures Staff.

Dedication
To the memory of my father, James Lee Ross,
And for my daughter, Lily Katherine Ross

Studio photography and book design by Robert Biondi.

Library of Congress Catalog Number: 2002101998.

Printed in China.
ISBN: 0-7643-1682-6

Published by Schiffer Publishing Ltd.
4880 Lower Valley Road
Atglen, PA 19310
Phone: (610) 593-1777
FAX: (610) 593-2002
E-mail: Schifferbk@aol.com.
Visit our web site at: www.schifferbooks.com
Please write for a free catalog.
This book may be purchased from the publisher.
Please include $3.95 postage.
Try your bookstore first.

In Europe, Schiffer books are distributed by:
Bushwood Books
6 Marksbury Ave.
Kew Gardens
Surrey TW9 4JF
England
Phone: 44 (0)208 392-8585
FAX: 44 (0)208 392-9876
E-mail: Bushwd@aol.com.
Free postage in the UK. Europe: air mail at cost.
Try your bookstore first.

CONTENTS

BROTHERS ALL

I am honored to write this brief dedication essay to tell what it meant, and indeed still means to me, to be a former U.S. Army Ranger. My fellow former Ranger friends and our few years of Ranger experiences in World War II were part of one of the most rewarding and exciting chapters of my adventuresome life. I'm now in my eighties, have a large family filled with love, and continue to enjoy a happy and healthy life. My good fortune is in many ways still connected to our Ranger brotherhood, and the closest bonding with men I've ever known.

The Rangers were a volunteer combat outfit of approximately five-hundred warriors in each of the six Army Ranger battalions of World War II. They were highly intelligent, honorable, reliable, resourceful, courageous men, whose common sense and good judgment enabled them to succeed at whatever they undertook to accomplish. We had the toughest training known to the military. Whether climbing high cliffs without safety ropes, or using explosives and live fire in realistic combat training, we placed our lives in the hands of one another.

As Ranger volunteers, we were given some of the war's most dangerous missions, from the perilous raid on Dieppe, France, to the pivotal battle at El Guettar, North Africa, to clashes in the trackless uplands and fortified villages of Italy. Other Ranger missions saved many lives, such as the destruction of the menacing coastal battery behind Pointe du Hoc, France, and the daring rescue of over 500 American PWs from the Japanese prison camp at Cabanatuan, Philippines. In invasions and campaigns, major battles and Ranger raids, we unrelentingly carried the war to our enemies until final victory was achieved.

We had high casualty rates. The horrors of war forged a unique and enduring Ranger friendship. I served in D Company, 2nd Ranger Battalion; we became a family of loyal brothers, all for one and one for all. For fifty-seven years so far, the surviving Rangers have been and continue to be my best friends. Their courage, good character, high integrity, self-discipline, hard work and dedication continued in their successful civilian lives. They are very patriotic good citizens. I am extremely proud of them all.

Our civilian organization, the Ranger Battalions Association of World War II, founded in 1948, still meets regularly. We remember respectfully our deceased buddies while reminiscing. They are always in our prayers. Our Ranger historians keep the record straight for interested family members and others. Our families stay in touch with each other. Ranger friendships are forever. Our dedication to duty and honor was indelibly imprinted on our hearts and minds. Our present day motto, "Rangers, Lead the Way!," was born on Omaha Beach on June 6, 1944, where Rangers were among the first to land, and among the first to die. Our present day Rangers are just as dedicated as we old Rangers. Their Ranger friendships are forever, too.

2nd Lieutenant Leonard G. Lomell, DSC
Toms River, New Jersey, August 2001

PART I

American Commandos: Training and the Early Raids

OPPOSITE TOP: B Company, 1st Ranger Battalion, led by First Lieutenant Alfred Nelson, on road march near Achnacarry, Scotland, July 1942. The story of America's World War II Rangers officially began in Great Britain on June 1, 1942, with the issuing of a letter from the Headquarters, United States Army Forces in the British Isles, to the Commanding General, United States Army Northern Ireland Forces, directing the immediate establishment of an American "commando organization." It would be called the 1st Ranger Battalion, Provisional. The name, 'Ranger', a uniquely American terminology that had arisen during the French and Indian War, was chosen for the new unit by Brigadier General Lucien K. Truscott, Jr. In April 1942, Truscott had been named United States Advisor to the Chief of Combined Operations (British), and it was on Truscott's recommendation, with the backing of United States Army chief of staff, General George C. Marshall, that the Rangers would be established. (National Archives, RG111-SC-142351)

OPPOSITE BOTTOM: Officers of the 1st Ranger Battalion pose in front of their quarters at the Commando Depot, Achnacarry Estate, near Spean Bridge, Invernesshire, Scotland, July 1942. Top row, left to right: Lieutenant Joseph H. Randall, Lieutenant Walter F. Nye, Lieutenant Robert Flanagan, Captain William E. Martin, Lieutenant James B. Lyle, Lieutenant Dean H. Knudson. Third row, Captain Stephen J. Meade, Lieutenant Frederick F. Ahlgren, Lieutenant Axel W. Anderson, Lieutenant Leonard F. Dirks, Captain Alvah M. Miller, Lieutenant Leilyn Young. Second row, Lieutenant Charles Shunstrom, Lieutenant Gordon L. Klefman, Lieutenant William L. Jarrett, Lieutenant William B. Lanning, Lieutenant Alfred H. Nelson, Lieutenant Robert L. Johnston. Front row, Captain Roy Murray, Jr., Lieutenant Edward V. Loustalot, Lieutenant Frederick J. Saam, Major William O. Darby, Lieutenant George P. Sunshine, Lieutenant Max Schneider, Captain Herman W. Dammer, Lieutenant Earl L. Carran. (National Archives, RG111-SC-142314)

ABOVE: Ranger volunteers use a log as a training tool, Commando Depot, Achnacarry, August 1942. The 1st Ranger Battalion would be set up along the lines of a British Commando. Per its table of organization, the battalion would consist of a Headquarters and Headquarters Company (eight officers and 69 enlisted men), and six Ranger Companies (each of three officers and 62 enlisted men). Very early on, the battalion's initial strength, 26 officers and 441 enlisted men, was increased to include a 10% overstrength of personnel in the grades of Sergeant, Staff Sergeant, and Technical Sergeant, ostensibly to assure availability of fitted personnel upon completion of the initial training period. Furthermore, it was stated in the directive: "As far as practicable, the American unit will be armed and equipped with the American counterpart of corresponding British items." (National Archives, RG111-SC-140983)

A candidate for the 1st Ranger Battalion trains on the 'bullet and bayonet' course at the Commando Training Depot with a British Commando instructor looking on, August 1942. While the 1st Ranger Battalion was to be a permanent unit, membership in its ranks, as a general rule, was to be on a temporary basis only. Under the direction of British Combined Operations Headquarters, the 1st Ranger Battalion was to be a "training and demonstration unit" – a mechanism by which maximum numbers of United States Army troops could gain valuable battle experience. At this stage of the European war, the Commandos were the only Allied military force carrying out offensive action on the ground against the Axis. Eventually, after the completion of a course of intensive and realistic training, newly-minted Rangers, alongside their British Commando counterparts, would graduate to undertaking actual raids. Thereafter, these combat-initiated Rangers would rotate back to their original units, and a new batch of select men would be inducted into the program. (National Archives, RG111-SC-140978)

A Ranger leaps from a twenty-foot barrier with full pack and rifle on the Commando Depot obstacle course, August 1942. A memo requesting volunteers for the new American "commando organization" was circulated to United States Army units then stationed in Northern Ireland. All personnel selected for duty in the Rangers were to be "fully trained soldiers of the highest possible type." It was required that officers and men alike possess inherent athletic ability, be able swimmers, have strong mental and physical stamina, a keen intellect, and personal initiative and leadership skills. While all volunteers to the Rangers would be subjected to strenuous physical conditioning and be required to qualify on an array of small arms, there were a number of specialized skills that were to be developed within each man. These included the art of self-defense, scouting and woodcraft, mountaineering, basic seamanship and small-boat handling, demolition and pioneer training, a basic knowledge of railway systems and locomotives, and an understanding of power plants and radio equipment. In the case of the two latter categories, this was so as to facilitate their destruction. (National Archives, RG111-SC-140986)

A Ranger Technical Sergeant displays small arms used by the 1st Ranger Battalion. Left to right: M2 60mm mortar, Boys .55" antitank rifle, M1 .30" rifle, M1919A4 .30" Browning light machine gun, hand grenades, M1903A3 .30" rifle with rifle grenade, M1918A2 .30" Browning automatic rifle, and M1 81mm mortar. The Sergeant holds an M1928A1 .45" ACP Thompson submachine gun. Commando Depot, Achnacarry, Scotland, July 1942. (National Archives, RG111-SC-142319)

ABOVE: Rangers and Commandos crossing a toggle rope-bridge, August 1942. By June 9, the first groups of officer prospects for the Rangers had been interviewed at locations in Lurgen, Omagh, and Wilmont, Northern Ireland. Conducting the interviews was, among others, Major William Orlando Darby, a West Point graduate and field artilleryman by trade, who had been selected to command the Rangers. The officers selected, twenty-nine in all, were detailed to duty with the 1st Ranger Battalion at Sunnyland Camp, Carrickfergus, Northern Ireland on June 10, 1942. In the complement were five Captains, thirteen First Lieutenants, and eleven Second Lieutenants. (National Archives, RG111-SC-140988)

OPPOSITE: Lieutenant William L. Jarrett, Ranger surgeon, trains at cliff-scaling alongside the rest of the battalion, August 1942. There were more than 2,000 enlisted men who answered the call for Ranger volunteers. An initial screening process disqualified most. Of the rest, 300 men from the 34th Infantry Division, arrived at Sunnyland Camp on June 11. Volunteers from the 1st Armored Division and other units arrived next day. Aside from infantryman, volunteers came from a cross-section of the American forces including field and coastal artillery battalions, quartermaster units, engineer outfits, signal corps and medical units, and so on. By June 14, a total of 575 enlisted volunteers were on hand. Over the next several days men underwent medical examinations, and personal interviews with boards of officers. Rigorous physical training and long marches were also meted out in an effort to further eliminate men with physical defects or lack of will. As a result, approximately 100 aspirants were found unsuitable and returned to their old units. (National Archives, RG111-SC-140974)

PRESTO
PAT. PEND
WALDEN

OPPOSITE: Mass hand-to-hand melee as a part of a general toughening up for Ranger volunteers. On June 19, by General Order No. 7, issued by USANIF, the 1st Ranger Battalion was activated. By June 22, when the final list of personnel was compiled, a total of 488 enlisted men had made the cut; twenty-six officers were present. The next five days were spent in issuing arms, equipment, and clothing in preparation for movement to the Commando Depot at Achnacarry, Scotland. In the midst of this, Brigadier Robert E. Laycock, commanding officer of the Special Service Brigade (British), accompanied by three of his staff officers, reviewed Darby's battalion, gauging its readiness to assimilate training. (National Archives, RG208-AA-42-R-2)

OPPOSITE BOTTOM RIGHT: M2 switchblade pocket knives. Though knives such as these are more commonly associated with U.S. paratroops, they were, nevertheless, listed as items of issue on some of the earliest hand-written Tables of Basic Allowance of the 1st Ranger Battalion, and are included herein for this reason. (Courtesy Joe Ranoia)

BELOW: After a tough day of training, Ranger Warren E. Evans lights a cigarette for one of the Commando Sergeants, August 1942. The 1st Ranger Battalion relocated to Achnacarry in three stages, beginning on June 28, and concluding movement on July 3, 1942. On Independence Day, 1942, training commenced at Achnacarry lasting through July 31, interrupted only by occasional inspection visits from various Allied General officers. Here, the Ranger companies were put under the command of British Commando officer-instructors assisted by one or more Commando NCOs (non-commissioned officers). According to James J. Altieri in his book, *Darby's Rangers*, the Rangers embarked on "the toughest and most realistic battle course to be taught at that time to United States troops. Coached by the Commandos, the Rangers soon learned what war was all about. Assaulting positions under live, direct fire, cliff climbing, swimming icy-cold rivers with full battle equipment, almost heartbreaking speed marches exacting all that human flesh and blood could endure; beach landings, fieldcraft, unarmed combat taught by some of the most competent instructors in the British Army: these were only some of the many courses in Ranger training. All training was on a competitive basis between companies. . . ." (National Archives, RG111-SC-140975)

OPPOSITE TOP: Under live fire carefully laid down by Commando instructors, a Ranger boat team splashes ashore during a training exercise on a Scottish lake, in August 1942. Live hand grenades were also used to simulate battle conditions. (National Archives, RG111-SC-140994)

OPPOSITE BOTTOM: A British Commando perched on a hilltop with a Bren Gun 'snipes' at U.S. Rangers making an 'opposed landing' during a training exercise. On August 1, the 1st Ranger Battalion moved to a new training station near Dorlin House, Argyle, Scotland, to undergo amphibious training administered by the British Royal Navy. Companies A and B bivouacked, according to the official history, at "Roshven, Companies C and D at Glenborradale, Companies E and F at Glencripesdale, and Headquarters Company at Salen and Shielbridge." Once settled into their new surroundings, the Rangers undertook landing exercises from a variety of small craft including "R boats, drifters, cobbles and cutters." (National Archives, RG111-SC-142324)

ABOVE: The Smatchet. Two U.S. manufactured examples of this heavy, cleaver-like weapon flank an example of British design. British Commandos trained with Smatchets and carried them into battle. It is very probable that some U.S. Rangers also acquired these ferocious weapons. (Courtesy Hayes Otoupalik)

BELOW: 1st Battalion Rangers clamber ashore from LCPs (landing craft, personnel) under simulated 'enemy fire'. Come September 1, 1942, the Rangers were once again on their way, this time to Dundee, Scotland. At Dundee the Rangers commenced with tactical problems under No.1 Commando, learning the methods to overcome beach obstacles, and to attack and reduce fixed fortifications including pill-boxes, anti-aircraft emplacements, and coastal artillery batteries. Battle was not far off. (National Archives, RG111-SC-140996)

Brigadier General Lucien K. Truscott, Jr. (center), U.S. Army advisor attached to the staff of Lord Louis Mountbatten, Chief of Combined Operations, and Major William O. Darby (pointing), inspect U.S. Rangers at Dundee, Scotland, September 2, 1942. Ranger Captain William E. Martin (standing at left) looks on. (National Archives, RG208-AA-3900)

OPPOSITE TOP LEFT: A U.S. Ranger (back toward camera) watches as wounded of No.3 Commando are dealt with aboard an LCM (landing craft, mechanized) immediately following their extraction from the French coast, after No.3 Commando's attempt to neutralize a German coastal battery complex northwest of Berneval-Le Grand, 4 1/2 miles east of Dieppe, August 19, 1942. (The Trustees of the Imperial War Museum, London, H 22615)

OPPOSITE TOP RIGHT: Wider view of Ranger and Commandos returning from Dieppe aboard an LCM. On August 1, when the bulk of the 1st Ranger Battalion was assigned to its training area near Dorlin House, Argyle, Scotland, a cadre of fifty select officers and men received orders to report elsewhere. Four officers and thirty-six enlisted men were assigned to train with No.3 Commando at Seaford, Sussex, England. Another contingent of four enlisted men were assigned to Lieutenant Colonel Lord Lovat's No.4 Commando, stationed at Portland, England. A third group of six Rangers, one officer and five enlisted men, were, on August 15, put on detached service to East Bridge House, near Farnham, England, with orders to report to an officer of the Royal Marines. These picked officers and men represented all six of the 1st Ranger Battalion's line companies as well as its headquarters company. (The Trustees of the Imperial War Museum, London, H 22617)

OPPOSITE BOTTOM: A trio of Rangers (Bill Brady is tallest man in center of frame) gathered on the pier after their arrival at New Haven, England, from the Dieppe Raid. This was the first time that American ground forces had been in action on the European Continent in this war. These Rangers are part of the four-man group that trained with No.4 Commando, rehearsing their attack plan in training areas around Weymouth, England, from August 2, to August 18, 1942. (The Trustees of the Imperial War Museum, London, H 22587)

ABOVE: At the port of New Haven, England, U.S. Ranger Sergeant Alex I. Szima has a light for his cigarette from a Commando. Another Ranger, Corporal William R. Brady, grins in background, center. The raid on Dieppe was, ostensibly, a reconnaissance-in-force aimed at gauging the German response, and as well as a means to test methods for carrying out a large-scale amphibious operation. No.4 Commando's assignment was to attack an enemy coastal battery, 1,100 yards inland, on the right flank of the landing beaches about one kilometer west of Varengeville-sur-Mer, and some five kilometers west of Dieppe. No.4 Commando's somewhat successful action at Dieppe was one of the few bright spots in an otherwise disheartening failure. (The Trustees of the Imperial War Museum, London, H 22580)

RIGHT: Arriving back at New Haven, five American Rangers dressed in OD herringbone twill work suits and carrying weapons and other equipment, wait to disembark from their LCP. Each raider was issued a British naval-pattern life preserver. Rangers armed with M1 rifles carried a total of 176 rounds of ammunition in a cartridge belt and in two cloth bandoleers. Additionally, each rifleman carried two No.36 Mills defensive fragmentation grenades and two No.69 bakelite fragmentation grenades, tucked into a meat can pouch attached to his belt. Demolitions kits made up of twenty pounds of assorted charges were carried in M1936 field bags or in M1928 haversacks. Some Rangers were assigned as riflemen, others mortarmen, Bren-gunners, or antitank gunners. Three Rangers in No.3 Commando's 3 Troop (pictured here) were equipped with an M1919A4 machine gun and 2,000 rounds of ammunition and ashore, it had been planned, would stay at the landing beach to defend No.3 Commando's 3-inch mortar section. (The Trustees of the Imperial War Museum, London, H 22603)

ABOVE: One of No.3 Commando's landing craft, LCP 44, with 1st Battalion Rangers aboard nears the quay at New Haven, August 19, 1942. The crossing of the Channel from England proceeded smoothly until 0345 hours when, while still approximately ten miles from the French coast, the small flotilla carrying No.3 Commando was taken under fire and scattered by a force of German E-boats and a flak ship, preventing many landing craft from reaching the beaches. Those raiders who were able to land at Beach Yellow 1 immediately came under withering small arms fire and a hail of grenades tossed by the German defenders perched on the cliffs. The few Rangers and Commandos who managed to survive the crossing of the beach and make it to the cliff top, were quickly captured. At Beach Yellow 2, one twenty-man boat team landed and, unopposed, moved inland to the rendezvous point near the objective by 0600 hours. Too small a force to attack the German battery, the Commandos and Rangers satisfied themselves by sniping at the gun crews until a withdrawal to the beach was effected at 0820 hours. (The Trustees of the Imperial War Museum, London, H 22605)

Word that U.S. Rangers had participated in the raid on Dieppe, France, spread quickly among U.S. troops throughout the British Isles. As the Rangers had no distinctive insignia, soon the bars of Britain resounded with tales of daring by would-be Rangers. In order to put an end to this, Major Darby ordered that a shoulder sleeve insignia be made. Pictured is First Sergeant Anthony Rada with the first shoulder patch ever made for the U.S. Army Rangers. His design won him six Pounds Sterling in a contest conducted by Darby. The colors, red, white, and black, the same as those used by the Nazis, were meant as a taunt to the enemy. (U.S. Army Military History Institute)

Corporal Franklin M. Koons, of Souix City, Iowa, is the first American to receive a British military decoration in the European Theatre of Operations during World War II. Corporal Koons was awarded for services at Dieppe, France, ostensibly for being the first United States soldier to kill an enemy soldier in ground combat in the ETO in World War II. (National Archives, RG111-SC-151645)

OPPOSITE: Sergeant Elias C. Petersen, 99th Infantry Battalion (Separate), shouldering an M1 rifle, Fort Snelling, Minnesota, December 1942. Early in 1942, numerous strategies for the Allied re-entry into Europe were under consideration by the Joint Chiefs of Staff. Among these was one which proposed an invasion of Norway, perhaps spearheaded by a crack unit of Norwegian-speaking commandos. Born of this contingency, the 99th Infantry Battalion (Separate) was activated at Camp Ripley, Minnesota, on July 10, 1942. To a man, officers and enlisted personnel were to be able to speak the Norse language. To that end, United States citizens of Norwegian extraction, and Norwegian nationals – aliens and aliens with first papers – were recruited. Many of the Norwegian volunteers were ex-merchant seaman whose ships had been lost to Nazi submarines; others of them had escaped the Nazi occupation of their homeland and had immigrated to the United States. The American volunteers came largely from the ethnic-Norwegian enclaves of the Midwestern United States. (National Archives, RG111-SC-169796)

BELOW: A Norwegian-American Sergeant of the 99th Infantry Battalion (Separate), leads his men in bayonet drill, Fort Snelling, Minnesota, December 1942. In late September the 99th Battalion moved to Fort Snelling, Minnesota and undertook training bent on winnowing out the unfit. On December 17, the battalion, 931 enlisted men and 36 officers, moved to the Mountain Training Center at Camp Hale, Colorado, and settled in to especially constructed barracks. For the next nine months the 'Norwegian Avengers' carried out a rigorous and comprehensive alpine warfare training program that included cross-country skiing, mountain climbing, and testing the Army's new T15 light cargo carrier. Challenged by the extreme cold that accompanied winter amidst the snowclad peaks of the Continental Divide, the battalion developed new methods for survival and battle-training that hinted at its future employment, and that would serve as a blueprint for other units to follow. (National Archives, RG111-SC-169800)

IGHT: 99th Infantry Battalion personnel train on the mounain obstacle course, Camp Hale, Colorado, 1943. Standard ıfantry clothing and kit was turned in, and the magnitude of ıountain equipment issued in exchange was staggering – nuch of it offered for testing by the War Department on a rial basis. Each man carried a cartridge belt, a gas mask, and rucksack. Attached to the pack was a rifle and bayonet, an ntrenching tool, a first aid pack, and three types of snowhoes: emergency, bear paw, and trail. Within the rucksack as stored white over-pants and over-mittens, tent poles and egs, a sleeping pad, climbers (to be added to the skis for steep lopes), extra socks and pocket insoles, 4-in-1 mountain raions, a canteen of water, and a change of underwear. Coleman as stoves, mountain cooksets, and mountain troop tents were ssued on the basis of one per two individuals. In the generous ockets of the ski parka, that every man was issued, was caried ski wax, a waterproof match box, spare mittens, wristets, goggles, and a mountain pocket knife. Topping off this aray was a pair of skis and ski poles. Individual loads ranged rom seventy to ninety pounds. (National Archives, RG111-C-1799

Personnel of the joint Canadian-American First Special Service Force learn how to properly exit a C47 when parachuting, Fort William Henry Harrison, Montana, Winter 1942. The First Special Service Force was activated at Fort William Henry Harrison, near Helena, Montana, on July 20, 1942, in conjunction with Operation PLOUGH, involving the development of an experimental snow vehicle to mount an audacious sabotage scheme aimed at crippling hydroelectric and oil producing facilities across enemy occupied Europe, principally in Norway, during the coming winter. The FSSF was a bi-national Canadian-American unit of approximately 2,400 men, commanded by the nimble-minded, energetic Lieutenant Colonel (later Brigadier General) Robert Tyron Frederick. The FSSF had a unique organization: A Combat Echelon comprised of three identical 600-man 'regiments', and a Base Echelon comprised of a 600-man service 'battalion'. (National Archives, RG111-SC-187744)

BELOW: Leather A2 flight jacket belonging to a member of the First Special Service Force's Combat Echelon. Note the Force's red spearhead insignia painted on the left breast of the jacket. In the event a man either left the Force, or was transferred from its Combat Echelon to its Base Echelon, his leather A2 jacket was to be turned in to the Force Supply Officer. (Courtesy Hayes Otoupalik)

First Special Service Force personnel learn mountaineering, vic. Helena, Montana, c. March 1943. Consistent with the Force's original intent, all of its men were relentlessly trained to be parachute jumpers, skiers, demolitionists, cold weather survivalists, and unarmed combat specialists. Ski training was administered by expert Norwegian instructors. The demolition of all manner of steel and concrete structures was learned with a variety of explosives including dynamite, trinitrotoluene, and a new, concentrated plastic explosive called Ryan's Special. Techniques to exist under sub-zero conditions were learned from instructors from the Army Specialist Corps. Dermont M. O'Neill, seconded to the Force from the Office of Strategic Services, taught the Forcemen his devastatingly effective form of self-defense dubbed the O'Neill Method, based on jujitsu, that featured kicks to the groin, and blows to the eyes and throat. (National Archives, RG111-SC-187838)

BELOW: Red, white and blue shoulder cords, manufactured of dyed parachute suspension line, were worn by First Special Service Force personnel as a part their service dress uniform. (Courtesy Hayes Otoupalik)

ABOVE: First Special Service Force enlisted man's crossed arrows arm of service embossed metal disk insignia, and officer's pierced arm of service insignia. The Force's crossed arrows insignia was inspired by that of what was then the recently inactivated U.S.S. Indian Scouts, a formation of the Plains War era. (Author's Collection)

BELOW: Overseas cap of Staff Sergeant Cyril V. Krotzer of Headquarters Detachment, Second Regiment, First Special Service Force. The cap is adorned in the red, white and blue piping denoting the Force as a separate arm of service of the U.S. Army. 'Sid' Krotzer was an early volunteer to the Force at Helena, Montana, and participated in all of the Force's campaigns until he was wounded during the operation to break out of the Anzio Beachhead in late May 1944. (Author's Collection)

ABOVE: U.S. parachute qualification badge with First Special Service Force wing backers, showing detail of both front and back. This insignia was worn by Force personnel as part of their service dress uniform. (Courtesy Hayes Otoupalik).

TOP: A para-ski trooper of the joint Canadian-American First Special Service Force cooks a meal in his mountain cookset over a gasoline stove during winter survival training in the mountainous terrain near Fort William Henry Harrison, Montana, winter 1942. Ski equipment and his M1 rifle are close at hand. Political factors brought about the cancellation of the proposed sabotage operations in Norway for the FSSF, but this, in turn, only caused the reorganization of the Force for a new role as assault infantry. To effect this, the Force added an amphibious landing capability, and to its relatively small numbers it added an inordinate abundance of automatic weapons rendering it, arguably, the most able infantry organization in the Allied forces during World War II. (National Archives, RG111-SC-C3126)

ABOVE: Ski goggles and Ulster mountain troop pocket knife of the type used by the First Special Service Force, the 99th Infantry Battalion, and the members of the OSS NORSO Group. (Author's Collection)

Major Randolph Millholland, at right, commanding officer of the 29th Ranger Battalion, Provisional, stands with Major General Leonard T. Gerow, left, commanding officer of the U.S. 29th Infantry Division, and Lieutenant Colonel Griffith, c. June 1943. Millholland was selected to command the new battalion after completing the British GHQ Battle School, in Durham, England. All prospects for the 29th Rangers came as volunteers and were subject to strict physical and physiological evaluations before being accepted. (National Archives, RG111-SC-217607)

Commando Lieutenant John Lee Warner instructs 29th Rangers on a firing range at the Commando Depot, Achnacarry, Scotland, February 9, 1943. The 29th Ranger Battalion, Provisional, was activated on December 20, 1942, at Tidworth Barracks, England, in response to a directive issued by ETO Headquarters. Formed around a cadre of three officers and fifteen enlisted men from the 1st Ranger Battalion, the new organization drew volunteers principally from the U.S. 29th Infantry Division. As the 1st Ranger Battalion had transferred to North Africa, the 29th Rangers were to carry out reconnaissance and raiding missions along the north European coasts under the direction of the British Commandos, and thus would provide combat experience to its members, who would then be returned to their parent organizations in due course. (National Archives, RG111-SC-180092)

This group from the 29th Ranger Battalion, Provisional, are training with their M1928A1 Thompson submachine guns in preparation for combat. Left to right: Private First Class John Toda, Sharon, PA; Private John Dorzi, Barrington, RI; Private First Class Jack Womer, Dundalk, MD; Private First Class Robert Reese, McKeesport, PA; Lieutenant John Dance, Beckley, WV; Corporal Dale Ford, Thurmont, MD; and Private First Class Manuel Viera, Cambridge, MA. (National Archives, RG208-AA-42R-5)

ABOVE: 29th Rangers learn how to disassemble a Browning automatic rifle, Achnacarry, Scotland, February 9, 1943. After initial training and a weeding out process lasting from December 1942, through February 1943, the 29th Rangers moved from Tidworth to Spean Bridge, Scotland, and began training at the British Commando Depot at Achnacarry House. The course lasted five weeks, and upon its conclusion, these Rangers were attached to No.4 Commando and carried out practice raids along the south coast of England. (National Archives, RG111-SC-180091)

OPPOSITE TOP: Captain John J. Carlos, Quartermaster of the Commando Depot at Achnacarry House, Scotland, with Private First Class Hugh Byrd of Martinsville, Virginia, who is with the supply section of the 29th Ranger Battalion, Provisional. The two are examining the British mountain climbing boots that are issued to the Commandos, February 16, 1943. (National Archives, RG111-SC-183212)

OPPOSITE BOTTOM: 29th Rangers board a cutter for boating practice on a Scottish lake, February 10, 1943. After completing training at Achnacarry, a small detachment of 29th Rangers, three enlisted men under command of Lieutenant Eugene Dance, were temporarily assigned to a mixed British-Norwegian Commando raiding unit code-named Northforce. With Northforce, Dance and his men participated in no less than four forays to the west coast of Norway to carry out reconnaissance missions and to conduct raids. The results were mixed due, in some cases, to poor initial intelligence. (National Archives, RG111-SC-180097)

"KS"
U S ARMY FIELD RATION
12-1 RATION
MENU No 3

OPPOSITE TOP: Staff Sergeant W.E. Hewitt of Silver Spring, Maryland, checks the battalion's daily rations with the aid of Corporal George J. Klaczynski of Baltimore, Maryland, in England, December 7, 1942. The 29th Ranger Battalion was composed largely of volunteers from the 29th Division, a Maryland-Virginia National Guard unit known as the 'Blue and Gray' Division. As such, most of the men in the 29th Rangers, too, were Marylanders or Virginians, though men from many other states were also a part of the unit. (National Archives, RG111-SC-181235)

OPPOSITE BOTTOM: 29th Rangers prepare a meal of 5-in-1 rations as part of a War Department field ration test during training in southern England, July 14, 1943. Left to right, Private First Class Leslie E. Bragg, Charlottesville, VA; Corporal Marcus P. Little, Jarret, VA; Private First Class E.J. Watts, Norfolk, VA; Private First Class Amoss, Baltimore, Maryland; and Staff Sergeant Charles E. Lloyd, Lansdown, Maryland. (National Archives, RG111-SC-181241)

Tracers fired from the Bren gun of a Commando instructor pierce the night sky as 29th Rangers make an 'opposed' landing during training in Scotland, 1943. The 29th Ranger Battalion moved from Achnacarry to Dorlin House in July 1943. It was from this location that a detachment of 29th Rangers carried out their most successful raiding mission. Their objective was to destroy a German radar installation on Ile d'Ouessant, a small Atlantic island off the coast of Brittany, France. In the process, the Rangers were to capture two German prisoners and to leave behind an American M1 helmet with "Maj. R. Millholland, U.S. Rangers" inked on the liner, along with a cartridge belt for the Germans to find as calling cards of a sort. (National Archives, RG111-SC-185023)

BELOW: The 29th Rangers carried out as realistic a training regimen as did the Commandos or the 1st Ranger Battalion before them. Evidence this training casualty of an invasion maneuver, Private First Class Henry Foman of Lexington, Virginia, being loaded on a stretcher into the back of an ambulance after getting too near an exploding half-pound TNT charge, August 1, 1943. (National Archives, RG111-SC-255679)

BELOW: 29th Rangers shove a Bangalore torpedo underneath a wire entanglement in order to breach this obstacle during a beach landing exercise conducted near Bude, England, August 1, 1943. The raid on Ile d'Ouessant got underway on the evening of September 2. In dories, the raiders crossed the Channel undetected. The raiders located the landing beach and put in opposite the radar station. With the enemy yet unaware of their presence, the Rangers used wire cutters to silently penetrate the deep barbed wire curtain guarding the station's control hut. Reaching the hut, one team of Rangers set explosives and then fired them demolishing one wall of the building and felling one of the masts. A sharp firefight then ensued as some twenty to thirty Germans boiled from the structure to be cut down by Ranger Tommy guns and white phosphorous grenades. The helmet and cartridge belt were left on the beach as planned, but no prisoners were taken. The Rangers then withdrew without casualties. (National Archives, RG111-SC-179521)

ABOVE TOP: Shoulder sleeve insignia of the U.S. 29th Ranger Battalion, Provisional. This tab was worn on both sleeves of the Rangers' field and dress uniforms, in the British style. Note that on page 35, Lt. Col. Millholland wears a 29th Rangers tab on the sleeve of his British-made ETO jacket, June 1943. (Courtesy Dr. Mort Cohen).

ABOVE BOTTOM: Variant pattern of the 29th Rangers tab with offset '9', but which is otherwise identical to the first example, is believed to have been issued to members of the battalion's C and D Companies, organized in March 1943, three months after that of the battalion's HQ and HQ Company, and it's A and B Companies. (Courtesy Peter J. Bonner)

29th Rangers maneuver toward an 'enemy' pillbox during a training exercise on England's Bude coast, August 1, 1943. Soon after the successful raid on Ile d'Ouessant, a 100-man Ranger raid was planned against the Pas de Calais, but was aborted. Though the War Department was solicited throughout September 1943, to make the 29th Ranger Battalion a standing organization, these requests were turned down, and the 29th Ranger Battalion, Provisional, was officially disbanded in England, on October 15, 1943; its men returned to their parent organizations. Thus, fulfilling the mission for which the provisional battalion was originally intended, these aggressive, magnificently trained men were folded back into the U.S. 29th Infantry Division where their mettle was later tested in the bloody and terrible battles for places like Omaha Beach, and St. Lô. (National Archives, RG111-SC-179524)

ABOVE: In February 1943, the commanding officer U.S. Second Army launched a short lived Ranger School of two weeks' duration, at Camp Forest, Tennessee. Left to right, Corporal J. Jaggie, Corporal M. Riesenberg, and Corporal Blake, fire small arms on the hip firing course at the Ranger School. (National Archives, RG111-SC-C3441)

INSET: Ranger shoulder sleeve insignia of the type believed to have been worn by volunteers to the 2nd and 5th Ranger Battalions throughout the duration of their training in the United States. Furthermore, some 'divisional' Ranger personnel, upon completion of their training, wore this type of patch below their divisional insignia. (Author's Collection)

Lieutenant W.E. Vazzana plunges the blade of an M1918 trench knife into his 'victim', Sergeant J.R. Compton, during a demonstration at the Second Army Ranger School, Camp Forest, Tennessee, February 11, 1943. (National Archives, RG111-SC-168644)

M1918 trench or 'knuckle' knife. Though not an item of standard issue, many such knives found their way into the hands of Rangers and other U.S. special operations soldiers. (Courtesy Hayes Otoupalik)

RIGHT: Major Charles R. Goodwin, U.S. 66th Infantry Division – divisional Ranger.

OPPOSITE: Ranger Certificate of Proficiency awarded to Captain Charles R. Goodwin of the U.S. 66th Infantry Division. Apparently, some U.S. Infantry Divisions training for combat in Europe selected certain members of their cadre for 'special' Ranger training before going overseas. One such example is shown here. Captain (later Major) Charles R. "Tod" Goodwin, who played professional football for the NFL's New York Giants in the 1930s, completed Ranger training as a member of the U.S. 66th Infantry Division at Camp Blanding, Florida, during June and July, 1943. While the certificate lists the various courses completed by Captain Goodwin, it is doubtful these courses were as rigorous or demanding as the instruction meted out to standing Ranger battalions. Likely, the men selected for these short 'divisional' Ranger courses were intended to bolster the combat effectiveness of their respective units with their newly acquired skills. This type of training should, however, not be confused with that of the 29th Ranger Battalion, Provisional, of the U.S. 29th Infantry Division, who received elite training in England from the British Commandos prior to D-Day. Note: There exist official Ranger certificates from the U.S. 34th, 36th and 81st Infantry Divisions, and other U.S. Army infantry divisions, among these the 2nd, 63rd and 88th are known to have organized their own 'Ranger' formations. (Courtesy Mike Marine)

BELOW: Divisional 'Ranger' certificate awarded by the U.S. 81st Infantry Division. (Courtesy Peter J. Bonner)

BOTTOM: Unofficial insignia of the divisional Rangers, U.S. 2nd Infantry Division. These individually hand-made patches were worn on the field jacket or service coat above the left cuff. (Courtesy Dr. Mort Cohen)

81ST INFANTRY DIVISION

WILDCAT RANGERS

WE RAID AND FIGHT, DAY OR NIGHT

Private First Class John L. Florez, Company C, 306th Engineer Battalion

having successfully qualified in the severe requirements of the WILDCAT RANGER training and having proved himself to be an outstanding soldier, is hereby designated as a WILDCAT RANGER on the Twelfth day of March 1943, at Camp Rucker, Alabama.

PAUL J. MUELLER,
Major General, U. S. A.,
Commanding

Ranger

Certificate of Proficiency

Capt. Charles R. Goodwin

having demonstrated proficiency in the particulars hereinafter set forth is designated a

Sixty-Sixth Infantry Division Ranger

PRIDE, SMARTNESS, SOLDIERLY ATTITUDE AND LEADERSHIP
EXEMPLARY CONDUCT
PHYSICAL CONDITIONING
HAND TO HAND COMBAT
BLITZ COURSE
OOBY TRAPS AND DEMOLITIONS
LLAGE AND STREET FIGHTING

INDIVIDUAL CAMOUFLAGE
CONSTRUCTION AND PASSAGE OF WIRE ENTANGLEMENT
SNIPERS AND INFILTRATION
PATROLS AND AMBUSHING
STALKING AND AMBUSHING TANKS
IMPROVISED BRIDGES AND USE OF TOGGLE ROPE

ED THIS 3RD DAY OF JULY 1943 AT CAMP BLANDING

MAJ INF
NSTRUCTOR

LT COL GSC
AC OF S G-3

MAJOR GENERAL
COMMANDING

PART II

Mediterranean Operations: North Africa, Sicily and Italy

OPPOSITE TOP: Men of the U.S. 1st Ranger Battalion en route to North Africa, carry out loading drills into LCAs (landing craft, assault), which are suspended in their davits. November 6, 1942. Designed by the British, LCAs measured 41ft in length; their wooden well sides and side decking armored to protect the four-man crew and the cargo of soldiers and equipment. Like their Commando counterparts, the Ranger organization was set up around LCA boat teams – a Ranger platoon of roughly thirty men with their equipment being the number that could be carried in an LCA. (National Archives, RG111-SC-165315)

OPPOSITE BOTTOM: On D-1, Rangers of Headquarters Company, 1st Ranger Battalion, review a relief map of the territory they plan to capture, lead by Lieutenant Lynn M. Olsen. Two companies would land in the harbor of Arzew and move to capture Fort de la Pointe. The balance of the battalion would land at Cap Carbon on the nearby coast and capture Batterie du Nord. (National Archives, RG111-SC-172538)

ABOVE: 1st Rangers climb over the railing of their transport and down into their LCAs during boat drill while en route to North Africa. These Rangers wore U.S. flags on their right shoulders so as to be easily identified by the French forces who occupied the coast where the landings would occur. Slung over the shoulder of the man nearest to the camera is a 60mm M2 mortar tube. (National Archives, RG111-SC-165316)

LEFT: An LCA loaded with British Navy sailors and a cargo of Rangers motors away from the side of its mothership. The original caption for this photo states: "Assault landing craft being lowered into the water to carry U.S. Rangers to Algerian shore. 11/8/42." November 8, 1942, was D-day of Operation Torch, the Invasion of French North Africa. The 1st Ranger Battalion assault waves boarded their landing craft and carried out the actual landing under cover of darkness, so the action pictured is more likely to have taken place several days prior to D-day or, perhaps, later in the day on November 8. (National Archives, RG111-SC-165314)

OPPOSITE: Corporals Robert M. Bevan and Carl Drost, cover the approach to the captured French artillery battery from their outpost overlooking the harbor of Arzew, Algeria. The two have erected an expedient field fortification by piling up loose rocks to form a shallow parapet. The Ranger furthest from the camera is shouldering an M1903A3 rifle fitted with a grenade launcher. Also notable is the 3rd pattern Fairbairn-Sykes stiletto sewn to the trouser leg of the Ranger nearest the camera. The graffiti on their helmets was probably chalked on to satisfy a whim of the photographer. (National Archives, RG111-SC-165327)

BELOW: 1st Rangers force open the door of a small building that is part of the enemy artillery battery overlooking the town of Arzew, Algeria. A and B Companies of the 1st Ranger Battalion slipped quietly into the harbor at Arzew in LCAs during the small hours of November 8, 1942. Much to their surprise they were able to land at the quay, and launch their attack before the enemy realized what was happening. (National Archives, RG111-SC-165307)

ABOVE: A Ranger mans his Browning light machine gun from a perch atop a reinforced concrete observation bunker at Fort de la Pointe, formerly manned by Vichy French troops, Arzew, Algeria, November 8, 1942. (National Archives, RG111-SC-165309)

BELOW: 1st Rangers stand guard over a water supply tank, adjacent to the gun battery sight captured during the attack on Arzew, Algeria, November 8, 1942. (National Archives, RG111-SC-165308)

Major General Terry Allen, commander of the U.S. 1st Infantry Division, third from left, confers with Rangers and French officers outside of his newly established North African command post, November 1942. Allan was a great proponent of the Rangers. 1st Ranger Battalion personnel include Captain (later Major) Stephen J. Meade, center; Lieutenant Colonel William O. Darby, third from right; and Captain Frederick J. Saam, far right. (National Archives, RG111-SC-150009)

OPPOSITE: Lieutenant Colonel Darby frequently used this motorcycle for duty trips in North Africa. He is pictured here in front of Arzew's City Hall, November 16, 1942. Note the M1903A3 rifle carried in the leather scabbard of Darby's motorcycle. Though there are claims that the Rangers preferred this somewhat outmoded weapon, it was, in fact, the highly effective semi-automatic M1 rifle that was the Rangers' mainstay. The Ranger with whom Darby is speaking carries a 3rd pattern Fairbairn-Sykes stiletto tucked behind his M1911A1 automatic pistol. (National Archives, RG111-SC-165324)

OPPOSITE OVERLAY: 3rd Pattern Fairbairn-Sykes stiletto of the type issued to members of the 1st Ranger Battalion who trained under the British Commandos in the United Kingdom during 1942. (Courtesy Hayes Otoupalik)

BELOW: Shortly following the successful landings associated with Operation TORCH, the 1st Ranger Battalion went into bivouac adjacent to the coast some two miles east of Arzew, Algeria, and began training in anticipation of future employment. Road marches were one of the more effective stamina building elements of Ranger training dating back to days in northern Ireland. Pictured are men of the 1st Ranger Battalion during one such 'speed' march, moving past the North African Industrial Petroleum Company, west of Arzew, December 5, 1942. (National Archives, RG111-SC-165000)

ABOVE: 1st Ranger mortar section passing through Arzew during one of the many conditioning marches. The group here is manhandling a handcart that contains a complete 81mm mortar along with ammunition. (National Archives, RG111-SC-164996)

At the same point along the Algerian coast as witnessed the landings of elements of the 1st Ranger Battalion during D-day of Operation TORCH, Rangers now practice beach landings from LCMs, December 20, 1942. (National Archives, RG111-SC-174331)

1st Ranger medic, Private First Class Thomas H. Prudhomme, dresses the blistered foot of a Ranger, following one of their grueling speed marches in North Africa on December 5, 1942. (National Archives, RG111-SC-164995)

Shrouded in white smoke, Captain Stephen J. Meade directs the positioning of his company ashore using an SCR536 'handie-talkie' radio, vic. Arzew, Algeria, December 20, 1942. (National Archives, RG111-SC-174332)

179195

1st Rangers move off the beach and up a steep embankment during assault training near Arzew. The Ranger closest to the camera carries a British toggle rope on his cartridge belt. On his haversack hangs an entrenching axe. Helmet liners, rather than complete steel helmets, are worn. (National Archives, RG111-SC-174325)

OPPOSITE BELOW: The battalion's assault problem carries it out over the hilly terrain inland from the Algerian coast, January 20, 1943. From February 7, to April 10, 1943, the 1st Ranger Battalion saw further combat in North Africa in Tunisia. At the conclusion of this battle, the Rangers opened camp at Nemours, Morocco. Looking forward to the invasion of Sicily, Darby was ordered to activate two additional Ranger battalions, the 3rd and the 4th. (National Archives, RG111-SC-179195)

ABOVE: In order to practice street fighting tactics as part of battalion maneuvers, a 1st Ranger assault section races through an Arab village, having swooped down on it from the overlooking hill, vic. Arzew, Algeria. At Nemours, Morocco, in April 1943, Darby built an exact copy of the Commando obstacle course, and set about recruiting men for the two new battalions. Using the men of the old 1st Ranger Battalion as cadre, and fleshing out all three organizations with fresh volunteers, the 3rd and 4th Ranger Infantry Battalions were activated a Nemours, on May 21, 1943. (National Archives, RG111-SC-172067)

BELOW: Lieutenant Colonel Darby rests and takes chow with the men of his battalion during a break in training. Note that 'El Darbo', as he was affectionately called by his men, wears British 'SV' boots, issued to the Rangers during their training phase with the Commandos at Achnacarry, Scotland. Also note that his helmet liner is of early 'transitional' design characterized by gray rayon web suspension, and rayon and leather snap-in sweat band. (National Archives, RG111-SC-169212)

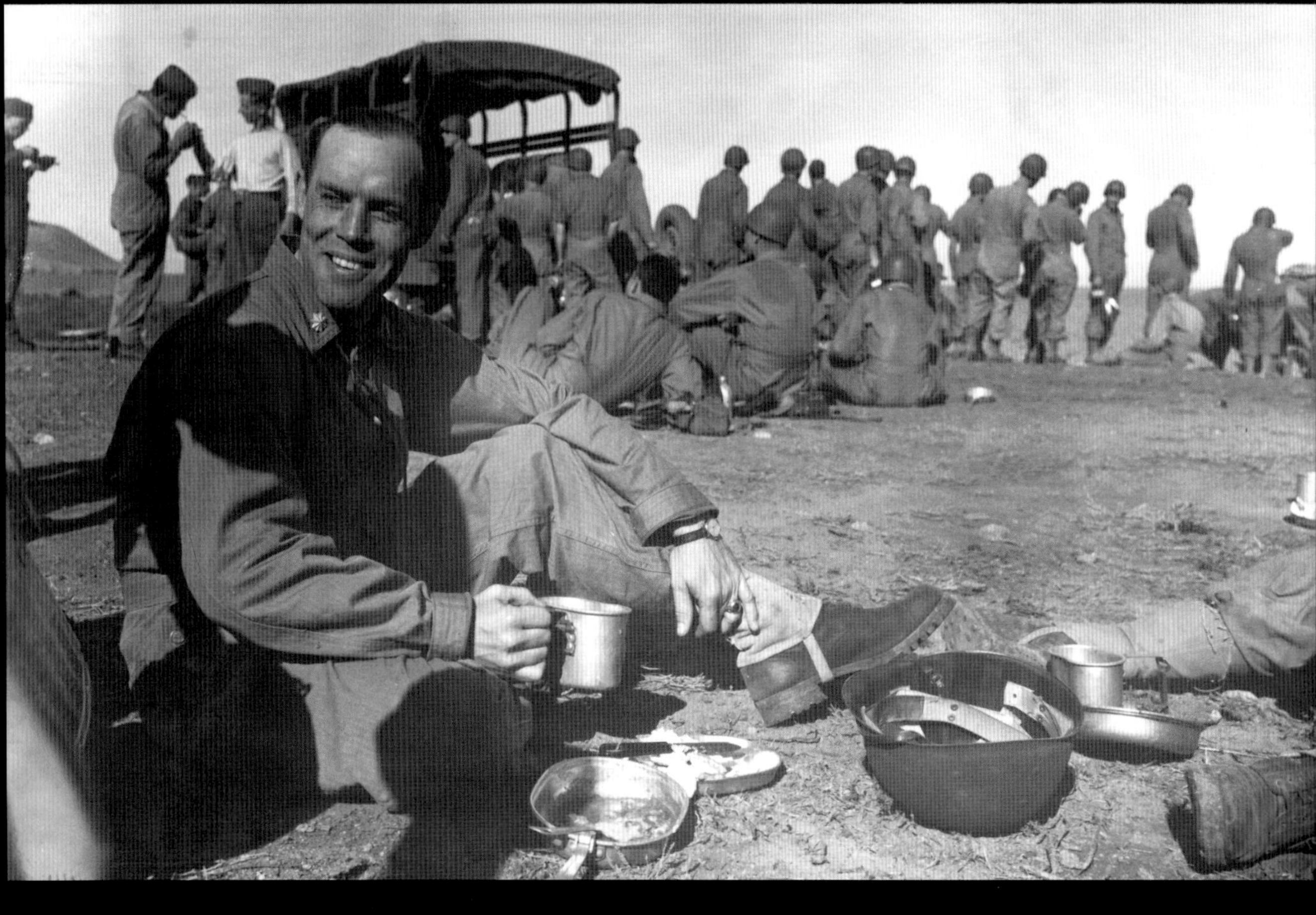

The 1st Ranger Battalion's enigmatic footgear: 'SV' boots. The Rangers of the 1st Battalion who trained under the Commandos in Scotland were each issued one pair of SV boots. The 'S' stands for sole, the 'V' stands for Vibram. SV boots were developed specifically for the British Commandos. The pair pictured were worn by Ranger Kenneth D. Gummel. The deeply cleated rubber sole was manufactured by "ITS-RUBBER CO LTD" of "ITSHIDE PETERSFIELD.HANTS. ENGLAND." The patent is noted as "DESIGN REGD 839218." The heel is constructed in two pieces: a cleated rubber heel attached to a thick leather midsection, all held in place by twelve metal screws. Twenty-two other screws join the sole to the midsole, itself of thick leather, running the full length of the boot. The uppers and toe cap are of 'rough out' russet brown leather, pebbled on the interior of the boot. The inside of the left boot bears the broad arrow mark with "WD" over "25" on the upper inside ankle. This mark appears on the inside of the right boot, too, only upside down. The padded leather insole is marked "UPSONS-DOLCIAN-LTD 1942 8 L." Each boot uses six pairs of brass eyelets, and the laces are woven, brown cotton, with crimped metal ends. (Courtesy Kenneth D. Gummel)

BELOW: The invasion of Sicily, Operation HUSKY, commenced on July 10, 1943. Private First Class Frank J. Tardio of the 3rd Ranger Battalion is credited as being the first U.S. Soldier to disembark and land on Sicily, at Licata. Tardio is pictured standing on the quay at Porto Empedocle, Sicily on July 17, 1943. (National Archives, RG80G-74390/CL41-28)

RIGHT: 4th Rangers, Sergeant Edward F. Coyle (left) and Sergeant Dominick Lamandre accept a pitcher of red wine offered by a resident of Gela, July 11, 1943. Shortly after midnight on the morning of July 10, 1943, the 1st and 4th Ranger Battalions made an amphibious landing to capture the port city of Gela, as the first step of wresting Sicily from the Axis. (Bob Landry/TimePix, Inc., 588119)

Lieutenant General George S. Patton, commanding officer of the U.S. Seventh Army, congratulates Lieutenant Colonel William O. Darby, commanding officer of the Ranger force, on his successful attack to seize the port city of Gela, Sicily, July 10, 1943. So impressed with Darby was Patton, that he offered the head Ranger the command of an infantry regiment and a promotion to full Colonel. Darby turned him down, preferring to stay with his Rangers. (Bob Landry/ TimePix, Inc., 612622)

Rangers and U.S. 1st Armored Division troops mill about on this Gela street shortly after the capture of the city. Some of the nearly 1,000 Italian prisoners, rounded up when the Rangers cleared the town in a house to house search using grenades for persuasion, can be seen seated on the front bumper of the M3 half-track at left. At 1000 hours on D-day, a small force of Italian light tanks crashed into Gela, but were driven off or destroyed by Rangers who blasted them with point blank bazooka fire, and who, from alleyways and windows, attacked them with sticky grenades and dynamite charges. A simultaneous attack by a regiment of Italian infantry was annihilated by Ranger and Chemical Warfare Battalion mortars. On D+1, a ferocious battle developed between the Americans determined to hold onto the city, and the Germans bent on driving them back into the sea. Elements of the crack *Hermann Goering Panzer and Parachute Division* mounted a massive effort to dislodge the Rangers, engineers, and chemical warfare troops holding the town. After a pitched twelve hour battle, the Americans, aided greatly by naval artillery as well as field artillery and self propelled guns – then just recently landed – succeeded in breaking up the attack. (National Archives, RG111-SC-175932)

SALONE
barbiere
Italol
MP

ABOVE: Loaded down with weapons and field equipment, Ranger infantry move up the winding road that leads to Chiunzi Pass. Darby's Rangers assaulted Salerno, Italy, on September 9, 1943, landing at Maiori, on the U.S. Fifth Army's left flank and then moved to occupy the dominating hills in order to prevent the Germans from launching counterat-

OPPOSITE: 1st Ranger Battalion First Sergeant Noland M. Gilbert of Mason City, Iowa, sharpens the blade of his M3 trench knife before going out on patrol. His M1928A1 Thompson submachine gun rests across his knee, c. September 16-19, 1943. (The Trustees of the Imperial War Museum, London, NA 7001)

U.S. M3 trench knife with M6 leather sheath.
(Courtesy Joe Ranoia)

OPPOSITE TOP LEFT: One of the 1st Ranger Battalion's First Sergeants, Howard W. Andre of Philadelphia, Pennsylvania, out on patrol in the rugged terrain of the Salerno Sector's left flank, c. September 16-19, 1943. In December 1943, Andre won a battlefield promotion to Lieutenant. He was later killed in action on the Anzio Beachhead. (The Trustees of the Imperial War Museum, London, NA 7000)

OPPOSITE TOP RIGHT: Smoke curls from the breach of his M1 Thompson submachine gun, as a Ranger fires on an enemy target, Tramonti, c. September 16-19, 1943. (The Trustees of the Imperial War Museum, London, NA 6998)

OPPOSITE BOTTOM: A patrol winds upward along a narrow mountain path, Tramonti, c. September 16-19, 1943. The man in the lead shoulders an M1 antitank rocket launcher. The others carry extra rockets either slung across their backs or, as in the case of one man, in an issue ammunition jacket. (The Trustees of the Imperial War Museum, London, NA 6997)

ABOVE: A Ranger patrol charges up a hillside under cover of smoke, Tramonti, c. September 16-19, 1943. (The Trustees of the Imperial War Museum, London, NA 6999)

Rangers of one of 3rd Battalion's special weapons sections (mortars) make a reconnaissance from one of the mountain paths on Mount Chiunzi, c. September 16-19, 1943. Note that the Sergeant at the left of the frame holds the base plate for a 60mm mortar, and is carrying the sight in its leather case on his left hip. Informed by Italian civilians that a party of the enemy have infiltrated into these hills, this group has gone out to make contact. (The Trustees of the Imperial War Museum, London, NA 6994)

Dust rises along the trail, stirred up by a patrol of the U.S. 3rd Ranger Battalion as it passes through a vineyard, many of which are scattered over the mountainside, c. September 16-19, 1943. (The Trustees of the Imperial War Museum, London, NA 6995)

U.S. 3rd Ranger Battalion shoulder sleeve insignia. (Author's Collection)

1 RANGER Bn
4 RANGER Bn

OPPOSITE: Lieutenant Colonel William O. Darby, CO of the 1st Ranger Battalion, and Lieutenant Colonel Roy A. Murray, Jr., CO of the 4th Ranger Battalion, confer over a map near Chiunzi Pass, September 18, 1943. Darby, while maintaining operational control of the 1st Rangers, was also commanding officer of ad hoc Ranger Force at Salerno, which included the 1st, 3rd and 4th Ranger Battalions, and the 83rd Chemical Battalion. (National Archives, RG208-MFI-5-U2) **OPPOSITE INSET:** Woven shoulder sleeve insignia of the 1st and 4th Ranger Infantry Battalions. These examples are both locally manufactured in Italy. (Courtesy Peter J. Bonner)

BELOW, INSET TOP: Cloth embroidered 83rd Chemical Battalion shoulder sleeve insignia. The first renditions of these unofficial SSI are believed to have been privately produced in Naples, Italy, in 1943. (Courtesy Peter J. Bonner) **BELOW, INSET BOTTOM:** Chemical Warfare Service officer's branch of service insignia, comprised of a Benzol ring superimposed over crossed chemist's retorts. (Author's collection)

BELOW: Tucked behind the ridge of Mount Chiunzi, a mortar team of the U.S. 83rd Chemical Battalion, attached to the Darby's Ranger Force, goes into action with their 4.2-inch chemical mortar, c. September 16-19, 1943. While the 4.2-inch mortar was originally conceived to fire screening, incendiary and gas shells, the advent of the 4.2-inch high explosive shell expanded the role of chemical battalions in World War II to include conventional fire support. Adding to the 4.2-inch mortar's appeal was its great mobility, accuracy, astounding range (nearly 4,400 yards), and the destructive power of its high explosive ammunition – nearly comparable to that of a 155mm howitzer round. While the Geneva Protocol for the Prohibition of the Use of Asphyxiating, Poisonous or Other Gasses, and Bacteriological Methods of Warfare precluded the use of such weapons in World War II, white phosphorous shells, intended for smoke missions, but which in addition inflicted horrific burn casualties, were not exempted. (The Trustees of the Imperial War Museum, London, NA 6996)

'Ike' jacket belonging to a former member of the 83rd Chemical Mortar Battalion. (Courtesy Peter J. Bonner)

BOTTOM: Hand embroidered variation of the 83rd Chemical Mortar Battalion's late-pattern shoulder sleeve insignia. (Courtesy Dr. Mort Cohen)

Enlisted man's overseas cap piped in the Chemical Warfare Service's blue and gold. (Author's Collection)

Close up view of a late pattern 83rd Chemical Mortar Battalion shoulder sleeve insignia, privately produced in Southern France, by a manufacturer of garment labels sometime after January 1945. This pattern, too, was unofficial and was 'approved' for local wear only. (Courtesy Peter J. Bonner)

Ranger Force headquarters personnel rest under an umbrella of grape vines trellised along the steep Tramonti hillside. Major William E. Martin (with telephone), Ranger Force S-2, receives reports via EE-8 field telephone about the accuracy of the fire by the Rangers' supporting artillery and mortars, September 18, 1943. Major Martin, joined the 1st Ranger Battalion in Ireland as commanding officer of C Company. During the North African campaign, Martin shifted to the battalion headquarters as Colonel Darby's Intelligence Officer (S-2). In Sicily he served as the 1st Battalion's executive officer before being assigned as the S-2 (Intelligence Officer) for Darby's Ranger Force for the invasion of mainland Italy. Later, Martin carried on as the S-2 of the 6615th Ranger Force, Provisional, at the Anzio Beachhead where he was killed by German artillery fire in January 1944. (National Archives, RG208-AA-9020)

A member of Darby's Ranger Force hands out C rations to Italian civilians, among them several children, who assisted in carrying supplies up the mountainside during the Salerno invasion, c. September 16-19, 1943. Note the shirt pocket that this Ranger has sewn to the front of his right pants leg, rendering them similar to British battle dress trousers. Photos indicate this practice was not uncommon among Darby's Rangers. (The Trustees of the Imperial War Museum, London, NA 7002)

Sorrento Peninsula, September 1943. Weary Rangers rest and smoke cigarettes behind a rocky overhang atop Mount Chiunzi. (Robert Capa)

Sorrento Peninsula, September 1943. A sweat-soaked Ranger rifleman organizes the contents of his cartridge belt and other equipment. (Robert Capa)

Sorrento Peninsula, September 1943. A lanky Ranger strides along a mountaintop trail shouldering an M1 2.36" antitank rocket launcher. This weapon, while not powerful enough to stop heavily armored vehicles was, nonetheless, very effective against bunkers and other fortified positions. (Robert Capa)

Sorrento Peninsula, September 1943. From atop a scrub-covered perch, a Ranger patrol peers over Mount Chiunzi's crest northward into the German-occupied valley below. (Robert Capa)

Sorrento Peninsula, September 1943. A wounded Ranger, his clothes and hair spattered with his own blood, is attended to by an aidman. (Robert Capa)

Sorrento Peninsula, September 1943. The fallen Ranger is removed from the field by his comrades. (Robert Capa)

Sorrento Peninsula, September 1943. The Ranger casualty is turned over to a party of litter bearers who carry him to the medical aid station inside a thickly-walled farm house near the top of the Chiunzi Pass. To the north, smoke rises from the

Sorrento Peninsula, September 1943. Interior of 'Fort Schuster' showing good view of Ranger Force command group, as well as members of attached units including elements of the U.S. 36th Infantry Division, and U.S. 504th Parachute Infantry Regiment, part of the 82nd Airborne Division. This former residence turned 'fort' was named in honor of Captain Emil Schuster, a medical officer of the 3rd Ranger Battalion, and served manifold purposes, as a medical aid station, a command post, and as an observation point to direct naval and field artillery, and mortar fire. (Robert Capa)

Sorrento Peninsula, September 1943. Lieutenant Colonel William O. Darby, head Ranger, looks over maps inside of 'Fort Schuster', near Chiunzi Pass. At Darby's left sits Lieutenant Colonel Fred L. Walker, Jr., commander of the 1st Battalion 143rd Infantry U.S. 36th Infantry Division, temporarily attached to Darby's command. (Robert Capa)

Sorrento Peninsula, September 1943. A fighting patrol from the 1st Ranger Battalion halted along a trail atop Mount Chiunzi. (Robert Capa)

OPPOSITE TOP: Elements of D Company, 3rd Ranger Battalion, pass a shelled-out dwelling en route to new positions atop a wooded hill at the front in the Santa Maria Sector, November 10, 1943. (National Archives, RG111-SC-178547)

OPPOSITE BOTTOM: Santa Maria Sector, Italy, November, 1943. Ranger rifleman of D Company, 3rd Battalion, laying down covering fire to support the advance of fellow Rangers. (National Archives, RG111-SC-178548)

LEFT: November 1943. Ranger medic, Sergeant Thomas Prudhomme of Natchez, Louisiana, treats a leg wound sustained by Private First Class John Brady of Fairmount, West Virginia, of the 3rd Ranger Battalion during a skirmish at the front. Santa Maria Sector, Italy. (National Archives, RG111-SC-212443)

Two Rangers cover the advance of fellow soldiers with a barrage of rifle and automatic rifle fire during an attack against the German lines in the mountainous Venafro sector of central Italy, c. December 1943. (National Archives, RG208-AA-19278-FO)

BELOW: 1st Battalion Rangers kneeling by their 81mm mortar on Venafro Ridge in December 1943. Left to right are Sergeant Arthur S. Wraa of San Francisco, California, Lieutenant Beverley E. Miller of New York City, and Sergeant Albert C. Kissman of Manchester, Connecticut. (Corbis, U708633ACME)

A special weapons section of D Company, 3rd Ranger Battalion, carrying components of a 60mm mortar and ammunition, moves into position down a narrow ravine at the Italian front in the Santa Maria Sector, Italy, November 10, 1943. (National Archives, RG111-SC-178545)

ABOVE: Two officers of 1st Company, Third Regiment, First Special Service Force rest near the Force clearing station at Le Noci, Italy, in January 1944. Seated at left is Lieutenant J. Kostelec of Calgary, Alberta, Canada. At right is First Lieutenant Howard C. Wilson of Olympia, Washington. The FSSF utilized a variety of winter equipment including the reversible parka as worn by Wilson. (National Archives of Canada, PA 128984)

INSET: Shoulder sleeve insignia of the First Special Service Force. Left and center, two variations of U.S. manufacture. Right, woven cloth example of Italian origin. (Author's collection)

BELOW: Canadians of Second Regiment, First Special Service Force, Radicosa area, Italy, January 16, 1944. Sergeant George Kulyk, far left, of Saskatchewan, Canada, and Lieutenant William S. Story, far right, of Manitoba, Canada, restore to the fold three former prisoners of the Germans, who made their escape together. From left to right they are: Timothy Alexcesia, Nov Sibersk, Siberia; Ehmatte Wemamen, Stalingrad, Russia; and Giuseppe Piusig, Trieste, Italy. (National Archives, RG111-SC-236355)

RIGHT: M1942 parachute jumper boots, worn by Sergeant Herbert E. Morris, Communications Sergeant, Headquarters Detachment, 1st Battalion, Third Regiment, First Special Service Force. Morris wore these boots with the Force during the liberation of Southern France and, with the U.S. 474th Infantry Regiment, Separate, during the occupation of Norway. (Author's Collection)

Darby's Rangers: Weapons, Clothing and Equipment

Based on Table of Basic Allowances, Ranger Battalion, 11 June 1942, et. al.

1st Ranger Battalion personnel who completed training in Scotland under the British Commandos were each issued a Fairbairn-Sykes fighting knife of either the 2nd or 3rd Pattern, the latter (1) being the most common. Per the 1st Ranger Battalion's original table of basic allowances, all Rangers were to be issued an M2 switchblade pocket knife (2). In Ranger companies the M1911A1 .45" Colt automatic pistol (3) with .45" ACP ammunition, two spare seven-round magazines (4) and an M1916 leather holster (5) was issued to machine gun and mortar crewmen, and to certain platoon and company headquarters personnel. The M1 .30" semi-automatic Garand rifle w/ M1907 leather rifle sling (6) was a Ranger company's primary source of firepower. The M1 accepted the M1942 bayonet (7) with M3 scabbard. Ammunition for the M1 rifle was held in eight-round *en-bloc* clips (8) containing either .30" M2 ball or .30" tracer ammunition. Clips for both M1 and M1903 rifle ammunition were carried in a web cartridge belt of either the 9-pocket M1918 'mounted' type (9) incorporating an M1918 double web magazine pouch (10) to carry automatic pistol ammunition or, more commonly, in the 10-pocket M1923 'dismounted' type. In addition to the clips each rifleman carried in his cartridge belt, six-pocket cloth bandoleers (11) containing six clips apiece were also distributed. The pockets of the cartridge belt could as well accommodate a tin of bore cleaner (12) if necessary. The .30" cleaning kit (13) was used to service rifles, automatic rifles and light machine guns alike. Depending on mission requirements, most Rangers in the fighting sections each carried up to six hand grenades (14) usually being a mix of U.S. MkIIA1 fragmentation, AN-M14 Thermite incendiary, and white phosphorous smoke, and British No.69 plastic charge fragmentation, No.77 smoke, and No.74 Mk2 sticky grenades. Grenades were most often carried in a meat can pouch (15) which was removed from the haversack and attached to the left side of the cartridge belt.

In a Ranger company, officers and NCOs at or above the rank of Sergeant were issued binoculars (16), the M2 luminous dial lensatic compass with waterproof case (17), and the 'thunderer' whistle (18) used for signaling. Rangers in the Mediterranean were issued M1A1 training gas masks with web cases. The masks were usually discarded, but the web cases (19) were retained as storage pouches for rations, ammunition or even cigarettes. The gas mask case, along with the M1910 entrenching shovel in its M1910 carrier (20) were attached to the M1923 haversack (21) shouldered by Ranger enlisted men.

On the cartridge belt was carried an M1910 canteen, cup and dismounted cover (22), and an M1924 first aid packet and pouch (23). Other equipment included a pair of M1938 wire cutters with M1938 carrier (24), a TL122A flashlight (25), a pair of Polaroid 1021 all-purpose goggles (26) and a 7 jewel wrist watch (27). The M1926 dual type life belt (28) was often used by Rangers during amphibious landings, worn under the equipment so that in the event of emergency, the equipment could be jettisoned and the belt inflated. Every Ranger wore an M1 steel helmet and liner (29). Early rations included C rations (30) and concentrated chocolate D ration bars (31). Each man was issued an M1926 knife, fork and spoon set (32) and a meat can (33). Personal items carried by Ranger personnel included a pair of identification 'dog' tags with necklace and extension (34), tent candles (35), a shaving kit and soap (36), a hard rubber comb (37), a toothbrush (38), an OD cotton handkerchief (39), and a lighter and/or waterproof plastic match box with matches (40).

The M1941 wool knit cap (41) was a popular and functional item of headgear. Among the various types of underclothes (42) were OD cotton drawers, wool drawers, cotton/wool blend undershirts, and OD cushion-sole light-wool socks. Outer wear included an M1937 web waist belt (43), OD wool serge trousers (44), an OD wool flannel shirt (45), cut down M1938 dismounted canvas leggings (46), field service shoes (47), and OD wool leather palm gloves (48). The M1938 EM's raincoat (49) worn over a field jacket was usually a Ranger's sole protection against the elements when under battle conditions. When in static positions, or behind the front lines, a Ranger would be able to retrieve his bedroll from unit transportation. Each bedroll consisted of a shelter half tent (50), five wooden shelter pins and tent rope (51), folding shelter tent pole (52), and one or two M1934 OD wool blankets (backdrop). Two Rangers, by combining the contents of their bedrolls were able to erect and share a shelter tent, using their raincoats as ground sheets and wrapping themselves in the blankets.

Also see plates on page 98.

FOXHOLE Lighter
U.S. G.S.M.CO. 1942
ITALIAN
FRENCH
NORTH AFRICA
GERMAN PHRASE BOOK
SOAP
FOOT POWDER
U.S.
27
52
40
34
33
18
32
50
37
51
43
36
20
38
39
25
41
35
49
7
28
2
1
3
30
42
4
26
8
10
12
9
23
14
31
22
5
24
48
16
17
11
6
13

See key on page 96.

Ranger Company, Ranger Infantry Battalion

Composite of Tables of Organization circa September 1942 - November 1943
Personnel, Weapons and Initial Combat Ammunition Loads

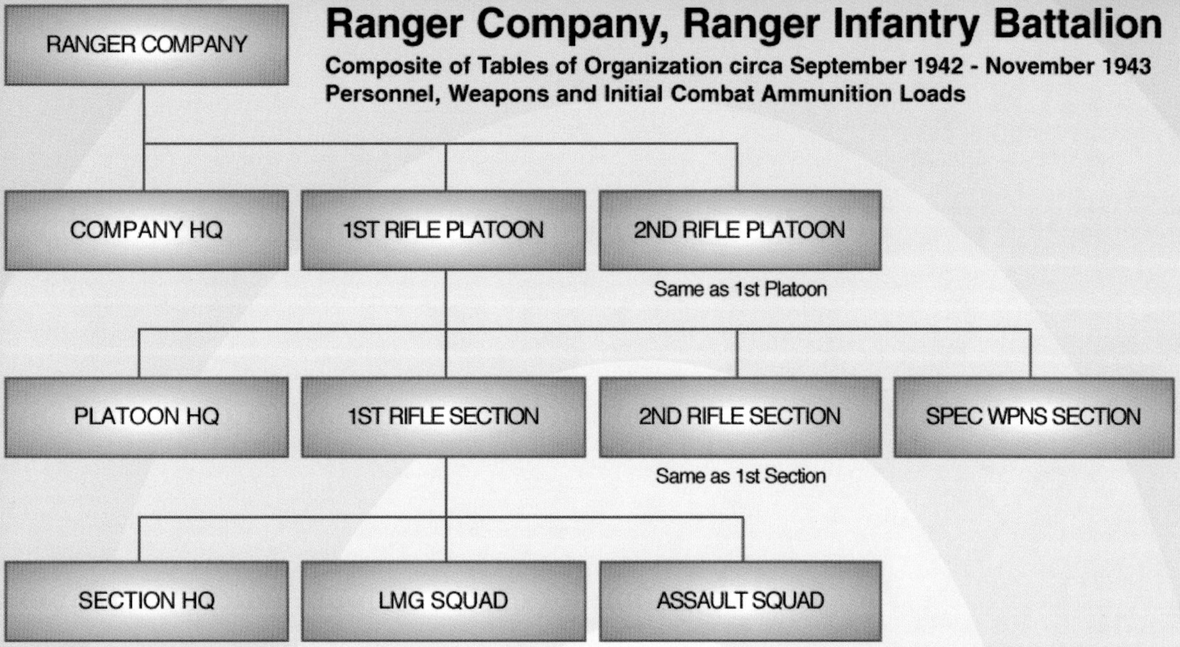

Each of the six standard Ranger Infantry Battalions was composed of a Headquarters and Headquarters Company, and six Ranger Companies. The firepower for the battalion resided in its companies.

Headquarters, Ranger Company
Captain, Company Commander, .30" M1 rifle and 10 clips (80 rounds), .45" M1911A1 pistol and 3 clips (21 rounds)
First Sergeant, M1928A1 Thompson submachine gun and 11 clips (220 rounds), .45" M1911A1 pistol and 3 clips (21 rounds)
Sergeant, Clerk, .30" M1 rifle and 22 clips (176 rounds)
Sergeant, Messenger/Grenadier, M1903 rifle and 20 clips (100 rounds), grenade launcher and 8 M9A1 antitank rifle grenades

Headquarters, Rifle Platoon
First Lieutenant, Platoon Leader, .45" M1928A1 submachine gun and 11 clips (220 rounds)
Staff Sergeant, Platoon Guide, .45" M1928A1 submachine gun and 11 clips (220 rounds), .45" M1911A1 pistol and 3 clips (21 rounds)
Technician 5th Grade, Sniper, .30" M1903A4 rifle w/ M73B1 telescopic sight and 20 clips (100 rounds)
PFC, Messenger, .30" M1 rifle and 22 clips (176 rounds)

Special Weapons Section, Rifle Platoon[1]
Sergeant, Section Leader, M1 rifle and 22 clips (176 rounds), mortar base plate and M4 sight
Technician 4th Grade, Mortar Gunner, .45" M1911A1 pistol and 3 clips (21 rounds), M2 60mm mortar tube and bipod
Technician 5th Grade, Assistant Mortar Gunner, .45" M1911A1 pistol and 3 clips (21 rounds), 60mm M49A1 HE ammunition (12 rounds)
PFC, Ammunition Carrier, M1 rifle and 22 clips (176 rounds), 60mm M49A1 HE ammunition (12 rounds)
PFC, Ammunition Carrier, M1 rifle and 22 clips (176 rounds), 60mm M49A1 HE ammunition (12 rounds)

Headquarters, Rifle Section
Sergeant, Section Leader, M1 rifle and 22 clips (176 rounds), 6 MkIIA1 fragmentation hand grenades

Light Machine Gun Squad, Rifle Section[2]
Corporal, Squad Leader, .30" M1 rifle and 22 clips (176 rounds), 6 MkIIA1 fragmentation hand grenades
Technician 4th Grade, Light Machine Gunner, .45" M1911A1 pistol and 3 clips (21 rounds)
Technician 5th Grade, Assistant Light Machine Gunner, .45" M1911A1 pistol and 3 clips (21 rounds)
PFC, Ammunition Carrier, .30" M1 rifle and 22 clips (176 rounds), 6 MkIIA1 fragmentation hand grenades
PFC, Ammunition Carrier, .30" M1 rifle and 22 clips (176 rounds), 6 MkIIA1 fragmentation hand grenades

Assault Squad, Rifle Section
Corporal, Squad Leader, .30" M1 rifle and 22 clips (176 rounds), 6 MkIIA1 fragmentation hand grenades
PFC, Rifleman, .30" M1 rifle and 22 clips (176 rounds), 6 MkIIA1 fragmentation hand grenades
PFC, Rifleman, .30" M1 rifle and 22 clips (176 rounds), 6 MkIIA1 fragmentation hand grenades
PFC, Rifleman, .30" M1 rifle and 22 clips (176 rounds), 6 MkIIA1 fragmentation hand grenades
PFC, Rifleman, .30" M1 rifle and 22 clips (176 rounds), 6 MkIIA1 fragmentation hand grenades

Enlisted Cadre

1 x First Sergeant	2 x Staff Sergeant, Platoon Guide
3 x Sergeant, Section Leader	1 x Sergeant, Clerk
4 x Corporal, Squad Leader	1 x PFC, Sniper
4 x PFC, Light Machine Gunner	2 x PFC, Mortar Gunner

Total Company Strength 66 **Aggregate Strength** 84

[1] Boys .55" antitank rifle may be substituted for M1 rifle carried by one rifleman of the Special Weapons Section as required.

[2] The LMG Squad may substitute .30" M1918A2 Browning automatic rifles for .30" M1919A4 Browning light machine guns. When employing the Browning automatic rifle, the Light Machine Gunner will carry for the BAR 11 clips (220 rounds), and a .45" M1911A1 pistol and 3 clips (21 rounds). In addition, the Assistant Light Machine Gunner will carry a .30" M1 rifle and 12 clips (96 rounds), and for the BAR 12 clips (240 rounds).

Brigadier General Theodore Roosevelt pins the Silver Star Medal on a dapperly mustachioed Captain Frederick J. Saam of the 1st Ranger Battalion, U.S. Army Corps of Engineers. Colonel Darby looks on. Masone area, Italy, January 5, 1944. On January 16, 1944, the 'paper' 6615th Ranger Force, Provisional, was formed for Operation SHINGLE, the amphibious end-run at Anzio. On that date Saam was transferred to Ranger Force Headquarters to serve as S-4 (Supply Officer). (National Archives, RG111-SC-188052-A-S)

Baia, Italy, January 1944. Surrounded by his comrades, a Ranger lounges on the road with his back propped up against the curb prior to boarding naval transports that will carry him and the rest of Darby's Ranger Force to Anzio, where they, as part of Operation SHINGLE, will spearhead an amphibious landing in order to outflank the German defenses at Cassino. (Robert Capa)

Baia, Italy, January 1944. A Browning automatic rifle team of the U.S. 1st Ranger Infantry Battalion. The Ranger at lef carries some 240 rounds of ammunition for his BAR in 12 clips carried in his magazine belt. His assistant, also wearing a magazine belt with extra clips for the BAR, carries a dozen clips for his M1 rifle in two bandoleers slung across his chest

Baia, Italy, January 1944. A Ranger gives cans of Borden fruit juice to an old Italian lady who has come to see the Rangers off on the eve of the Anzio operation. (Robert Capa)

Baia, Italy, January 1944. A Italian girl has attracted the attention of two Rangers. Many local civilians, out of hunger, ventured into the Ranger staging area in order to collect what rations the departing Rangers might offer. (Robert Capa)

OPPOSITE TOP: First Lieutenant George B. Nunnally, commanding officer of C Company, 4th Ranger Battalion, checks his Rangers against the company roll as they pass to board naval transports at Baia, Italy. Earlier, Nunnally was wounded at Castellamare, Salerno Beachhead, and won Silver Star during the same action. Later, at Cisterna, he was killed while leading an attack against an enemy strongpoint. (National Archives, RG111-SC-187081)

OPPOSITE BOTTOM: Sailing northward toward Anzio, Italy, aboard the naval transport *Winchester Castle* on the eve of Operation SHINGLE, Captain S.F. Newdigate, commander of the vessel, looks on as Lieutenant Colonel William P. Yarborough, CO of the 509th Parachute Infantry Battalion, and Lieutenant Colonel Roy A. Murray, CO of the 4th Ranger Battalion, study a model of the beach where their troops are to land. Yarborough's paratroopers were assigned operationally to Colonel Darby's 6615th Ranger Force, Provisional, for this operation. (National Archives, RG111-SC-186957)

January 1944. Shipboard, Rangers review maps whist en route to Anzio. The 'V's and other lettering taped or painted on the backs of the Rangers' helmets are intended as night recognition markings so that patrol members might follow each other more easily. This was a practice that started with the Rangers during their actions in the Winter Line Campaign, November through January 1944. (Robert Capa)

Anzio, Italy, January 22, 1944. The Allied landing at Anzio-Nettuno was a nearly complete surprise to the Germans. During the lull that immediately followed their coming ashore, Rangers kill time by smoking and consuming canned rations. (Robert Capa)

January 1944. Colonel Darby and another Ranger hunkered down in tall grass at Anzio. (Robert Capa)

British General Sir Harold R.L.G. Alexander (pointing), commander of the Allied Central Mediterranean Force, chats with American Rangers beside a bomb-blasted building during an inspection trip of the new Allied front at Anzio. U.S. Rangers and Commandos, their British counterparts, made up the initial waves in the landings at Anzio which occurred on January 22, 1944. (National Archives, RG208-AA-22709-PNT)

ABOVE: British Commandos and a patrol of the U.S. 4th Ranger Battalion meet on the Anzio-Rome road. Elements of the 1st and 3rd Ranger Battalions of Colonel William O. Darby's Ranger Force had, on the night of 29/30 January, set out on the mission of capturing the important crossroads town of Cisterna di Littoria, which lay astride Highway 7 (the Appian Way), one of the principal arteries leading to Rome. Infiltrating toward the town up the deep irrigation ditches, the Rangers were to seize the town in advance of a heavier follow-up force from the U.S. 3rd Division. Disaster struck when at dawn on the 30th, these Rangers ran headlong into fresh troops of a German panzer grenadier division that had just arrived on the front. Outgunned, surrounded, and eventually overwhelmed, of the 767 Rangers who attacked Cisterna, only six exfiltrated back to friendly lines. (The Trustees of the Imperial War Museum, London, NA 11324)

OPPOSITE TOP: Rome, Italy, February 1, 1944. Darby's Rangers captured at Cisterna, Italy, are marched past the Colosseum by their German captors. Newsreel motion pictures were taken during this march to be shown in Berlin, demonstrating that German forces had captured the American 'cream of the crop'. Germany was rapidly loosing the war, but victories in battle, such as that at Cisterna, were exploited to prop up the morale of the German people. (The Trustees of the Imperial War Museum, London, MH 6338)

OPPOSITE BOTTOM: View of a 60mm mortar position operated by a crew from 3rd Company, First Regiment, First Special Service Force at the Anzio Beachhead in April 1944. Left to right, Sergeant Leonard L. Grew, Private J.F. Ball, and Private F.A. Murphy. Note the leather carrying case for the mortar's sight at right in the pit. The pit itself is dug deep and shored with heavy wooden timbers. (National Archives of Canada, PA 183863)

The Force's Johnny On the Spot

The First Special Service Force had serious need for a lightweight machine rifle, of characteristics similar to the Browning automatic rifle, and that could be carried with airborne troops in parachute operations. The Force's Canadian officers suggested adopting their beloved Bren light machine gun, but as it was chambered in .303 caliber rather than the U.S. Army's standard .30 caliber this made that choice impractical. However, a highly successful solution was found.

Produced by the Cranston Arms Company of Providence, Rhode Island, the .30 caliber M41 Johnson light machine gun met the qualifications. The Johnson was fitted with a folding bipod, and employed, conjointly, a conventional twenty-round detachable box magazine that fed in from the left side, with a five-round rotary internal magazine. Another of the Johnson's design innovations allowed for the magazine to be topped-off while remaining affixed to the weapon, by either loose rounds or by five-round chargers. Additionally, the weapon was fitted with a grip safety. From a closed bolt the weapon could fire single shots. From an open bolt the weapon could be operated on full-automatic with a selective rate of fire – 300 or 900 rounds per minute. The weight of the M41 with full magazine was approximately fourteen pounds in contrast to the approximately twenty-three pounds of the Browning automatic rifle and twenty-six pounds of the Bren Gun; and it could be broken down into three pieces for a maximum length of approximately twenty-two inches permitting it to be parachuted in the same manner as the M1 rifle. The lightness in weight and ease of assembly (from 20-50 seconds) made it an extremely valuable parachutist's weapon. Its high volume of fire made it perfect as a small unit support weapon.

An agreement was reached whereby 125 Johnson light machine guns, complete with accessories, spare parts and barrels, and instruction manuals were, in May 1943, delivered to the First Special Service Force from those procured by the U.S. Marine Corps from the frozen stocks of the Netherlands Purchasing Commission. In return for the 'Johnny Guns,' the Marine Corps was furnished by the Force with a quantity of the its newly developed RS explosive, that the Force had on hand in abundance. Each of the Force's 108 combat sections was allocated one Johnson light machine gun. Those M41s retained by the U.S. Marine Corps found use with their airborne units, and some Johnsons even found their way into the hands of British Special Operations Executive agents in Europe. However, the M41 Johnson light machine gun was never officially adopted by either the United States Marine Corps or the United States Army. (Courtesy the United States Army Ordnance Museum)

OPPOSITE: Private W.P. Lelievre, right, and Private L.E. Roussy, both of 5th Company, Third Regiment, First Special Service Force, inspect an M1941 Johnson light machine gun, April 1944. (National Archives of Canada, PA 183867)

ABOVE: As darkness descends, members of a fighting patrol from 5th Company, Second Regiment, First Special Service Force, cradling submachine guns, prepare to set off into no-man's land in search of the enemy. Forcemen were very adept night fighters, blackening their faces and hands to effect camouflage. This practice sparked the Force's nickname, *Black Devils*. Their helmets were also streaked with mud or grease paint to break up the familiar outline. Left to right, Sergeant Charles Shepard, Lieutenant H.H. Raynor, and Private First Class James A. Jones, Anzio, Italy, April 1944. (National Archives of Canada, PA 183870)

OPPOSITE: Private First Class Edward J. Wall, Jr., of Albany, New York, formerly a member of the 4th Ranger Infantry Battalion, now serving with Headquarters Detachment, 1st Battalion, Second Regiment of the Canadian-American First Special Service Force. Wall is pictured deep in Anzio's no-man's land, on the right flank of the beachhead, just before his unit is to withdraw back to friendly lines behind the Mussolini Canal after carrying out a successful raid against German forces around Cerreto Alto, April 15, 1944. (National Archives, RG111-SC-189498)

OPPOSITE INSET: *The Worst is Yet To Come!* Forcemen pasted stickers like these onto doors, fence posts, and even on the bodies of enemy dead as a method of conducting Psychological warfare. (Courtesy Hayes Otoupalik/Author's Collection)

USA
CANADA
DAS
DICKE
ENDE
KOMMT
NOCH!
USA
CANADA

ABOVE: During the early morning hours of 15 April 1944, Second Regiment, FSSF (minus one company), led by Lieutenant Colonel Robert S. Moore, raided German defensive works in the area from Cerreto Alto to the sea, and along the Strada Litoranea. Supporting Moore were H Company, 1st Armored Regiment; A and D Companies, 81st Reconnaissance Battalion; and one platoon from B Company, 701st Tank Destroyer Battalion. The raid was most successful, netting one officer and 43 men of the German *2nd Battalion, 735th Grenadier Regiment*, and 17 men of the Italian *Barbarigo Battalion (Light)* of the *San Marco Marine Regiment*. U.S. losses in personnel and equipment totaled one man slightly wounded, two medium tanks destroyed, and two tank destroyers and one armored car damaged. Sergeant Maurice Parker, Headquarters Detachment, 2nd Battalion, Second Regiment, First Special Service Force, trains a seized Walther 9mm P38 pistol on two prisoners captured during the raid. Parker also carries a .45" ACP Thompson M1A1 submachine gun in his right hand. Additional 30-round magazines for the Thompson are carried in an issue magazine case slung over his shoulder. (National Archives, RG111-

LEFT: Perhaps no article of equipment is as synonymous with the First Special Service Force as its stiletto, the V42, each individually hand-made by W.R. Case & Sons Cutlery Company of Bradford, Pennsylvania. Production began in November 1942, and in total, Case produced an estimated 3,500 V42s. The first 1,750 were procured for the First Special Service Force, and of these the first 500 were individually numbered. The horsehide sheath that came with each knife had an especially long belt frog, designed this way so that the knife might hang below the tail of the long ski parkas worn by the Forcemen. (Courtesy Hayes Otoupalik)

BELOW: From right to left, Brigadier General Robert Tyron Frederick, commanding officer of the First Special Service Force; Lieutenant General Mark W. Clark, U.S. Fifth Army commander; Brigadier General Donald W. Brann; and Major General Geoffrey Keyes, U.S. II Corps commander, study situation maps on the outskirts of Rome, June 4, 1944. The FSSF spearheaded Fifth Army's drive to capture the Eternal City. Frederick is shown carrying one of three original prototype Case V42 fighting knives delivered to the Force, distinguishable from the standard pattern by its bright stainless steel hilt and fittings. (National Archives)

ABOVE: Members of Major Edward H. Thomas' Headquarters Detachment, 1st Battalion, Second Regiment, FSSF, hurry past a burning German Mark VI tank during the capture of Rome, July 4, 1944. Tasked with the job of securing intact the Tiber River bridges in the northern half of the city, First Special Service Force was the first Allied unit to enter Rome in strength. (National Archives, RG111-SC-191061)

BELOW: Determined to carry on the fight with any means at their disposal, this guerrilla band, composed of American Rangers, South Africans, Russians and Poles, operated behind German lines in Italy, harassing the enemy and disrupting his communications. All escaped a German prison train at Plato, Italy. Standing second from right is Staff Sergeant Robert J. Taylor, formerly of the 3rd Ranger Battalion, who escaped from the Germans after being captured at Cisterna, Italy, on January 29, 1944. (National Archives, RG111-SC-220857)

ABOVE: After successfully linking up with U.S. forces north-east of Rome at Campagnatico, Italy, on June 21, 1944, Staff Sergeant Robert J. Taylor and his group are questioned by Fifth Army officers about their experiences behind enemy lines. (National Archives, RG111-SC-220860)

BELOW: Ranger officers – ex-prisoners of war en route to the United States – return to Cisterna, Italy, the site of their capture. They were liberated in Poland by advancing Russian troops. March 29, 1945. (National Archives, RG111-SC-387179)

PART III

Operations in Northwest Europe and Southern France

OPPOSITE: Men of B Company, 2nd Ranger Battalion, receiving haircuts at their marshaling area in England, only days before they will spearhead the invasion of France at Normandy – Operation OVERLORD. Rangers include, from left to right, Sergeant Joseph W. Shedaker, Private First Class Robert D. Herlihy, Private First Class James L. Roush, Private First Class William E. Gower, Technician 5th Grade Elmer P. Olander, Technician 5th Grade Charles J. Bramkamp (barber), Private First Class Kenneth W. Davis, and Staff Sergeant Paul L. Shave. The graffiti that adorns Olander's field jacket is worth noting as such was unusual during this time. Weapons, equipment, and an assault jacket lay scattered on the ground. (National Archives, RG111-SC-C1075)

ABOVE: Close-up of Ranger comrades Bramkamp and Olander jesting for the camera, each oblivious to his D-Day fate. Both men were cut down by the murderous enemy fire that greeted B Company when it was put ashore at the eastern edge of Dog Green Sector of Omaha Beach. (National Archives, RG111-SC-C691)

LEFT: M1941 field jacket with Ranger battalions shoulder sleeve insignia. (Courtesy Joe Ranoia)

ABOVE: 2nd Ranger Battalion personnel file along the waterfront at Weymouth, Dorset, England, on June 1, 1944, carrying full assault regalia, including numerous five-foot lengths of Bangalore torpedoes shouldered by men in the group nearest to the camera. The 2nd Ranger Infantry Battalion was officially activated at Camp Forest, Tennessee on April 1, 1943, and before war's end would participate in five campaigns. (National Archives, RG111-SC-C727)

BELOW: On the seafront at Weymouth, Dorset, England, U.S. Rangers enter a Red Cross coffee stall that serves also as the final checkpoint for unit rosters before the men move to the quay to board landing craft that will ferry them out into the harbor to, in turn, board the seagoing transport vessels. (National Archives, RG111-SC-C1217)

FOUR PHOTOGRAPHS - ABOVE AND PAGES 126-127: Personnel of the U.S. 5th Ranger Infantry Battalion begin boarding LCAs at Weymouth, southern England, on D-5. The 5th Ranger Battalion was activated five months after the 2nd Rangers in the United States, at Camp Forest, Tennessee, September 1, 1943.

RIGHT: Rear view of helmet of U.S. 5th Ranger as worn during the D-Day landings. This example was among the personal effects belonging to the family of a Private First Class in E Company, who was killed in action as a result of receiving a gunshot wound to the chest on December 2, 1944, near Carling, France. (Courtesy Joe Ranoia)

US 87
84
US
LCA
LCA
LCA 50

84
US 87
LCA
LCA

LCAs, tightly packed gunwale to gunwale with men of the U.S. 2nd Ranger Battalion, lie in Weymouth Harbor, England, on June 1, 1944, in preparation for transferring these assault troops to the larger transports that will carry them across the English Channel for the invasion of German occupied France. One may note that cleaning rods protrude from the barrels of some of these Rangers' M1 rifles, ostensibly to keep the barrels free of the damp, salty sea air, and other fouling. (National Archives, RG111-SC-190375)

Views of khaki 'assault jacket' of the type worn by 2nd and 5th Battalion Rangers during the D-Day landings. This jacket – more aptly described as a vest – provided the wearer ample storage for rations, ammunition and grenades within its generous pockets. The two quick release straps at the front of the jacket were designed so that it could be swiftly jettisoned if a man found himself struggling under the weight of the jacket's contents and in peril of drowning in the surf. (Courtesy Hayes Otoupalik)

Interior and exterior views of OD cloth assault jacket. (Courtesy Hayes Otoupalik)

Close-up of grinning Rangers seated in an LCA at Weymouth, on June 1, 1944. The Ranger at left holds an M1 antitank rocket launcher. (National Archives, RG111-SC-C739)

ABOVE: This view of the same group of Rangers shows a complete M2 60mm mortar lashed to the deck side at the upper left of the frame. (National Archives, RG111-SC-C741)

BELOW: Two LCAs leave the pier and begin the trip to the transport vessels anchored in the deeper water of Weymouth Harbor. (National Archives, RG111-SC-C729)

ABOVE: LCAs bearing U.S. Rangers speed into Weymouth Harbor to deposit their human cargoes aboard larger transport ships. Once loading is accomplished, the LCAs will then be hoisted into davits aboard these motherships and borne across the English Channel where they will then be used to carry out the landing operation. (National Archives, RG111-SC-C1090)

BELOW: British-crewed LCA 1377, carrying U.S. Ranger officers and men, moving out into deep water at Weymouth Harbor, England, June 1, 1944. This close-up affords one a detailed view of the armored ramp, well sides, side decking, and crew stations. (National Archives, RG111-SC-C1087)

ABOVE: Men of the U.S. 2nd Ranger Battalion manning an M1919A4 light machine gun in a defensive position near Colonel James E. Rudder's command post atop Pointe du Hoc, Normandy, France, c. June 6-8, 1944. The D-Day objective of D, E and F Companies, 2nd Ranger Battalion, was to land at the base of the Pointe, scale the cliff, and destroy the enemy shore battery complex located there. Gaining the clifftop, the Rangers found that the guns had been removed from their casemates. Later that morning, the guns were located, remarkably unattended, in an alternate firing position inland, where D Company Rangers, First Sergeant Leonard G. Lomell and Staff Sergeant Jack E. Kuhn, put them out of commission using Thermite grenades. Of the 225 Rangers who came ashore at the Pointe at H-hour, only ninety were able to fight by D-Day night. (National Archives, RG111-SC-320894)

LEFT: Rear view of M1 helmet as worn by an enlisted member of the U.S. 2nd Ranger Infantry Battalion during the D-Day landings. Stamped on the chin strap webbing on the left side of the helmet is "S-8433" – the 'S' standing for the first letter of the soldier's last name, and the digits being the last four of the soldier's serial number – suggesting that this helmet may have belonged to D Company Ranger Dominick J. Sparaco. (Courtesy of Mike Marine)

ABOVE: Colonel James Earl Rudder, commanding officer of the 2nd Ranger Battalion, and overall commander of the Provisional Ranger Group for Operation OVERLORD, at his command post near the tip of Pointe du Hoc, Normandy, France, on D+2. The signal lamp, to Rudder's right, was operated by Ranger Louis F. Lisko to call for supporting naval artillery fire from the several destroyers offshore, thus helping to break up German attempts to eject the Rangers from their lodgment. (U.S. Army Military History Institute)

OPPOSITE TOP: Just a few days after the invasion, an LCVP (landing craft, vehicle, personnel) lands supplies and extricates wounded across the rocky, shell cratered shingle skirting Pointe du Hoc, France. Strewn over the beach are some of the grapnel-tipped rope ladders and toggle ropes that were intended to be hung by rockets from the cliff top to aid the Rangers in their ascent. These craters proved to be one of the unforeseen hazards of the D-Day landing at the Pointe; some Rangers stepping out of their landing craft suddenly found themselves struggling to climb free of these wells, all while soaked to the skin, heavily laden with equipment, possibly seasick, and under intense enemy small arms fire. (National Archives, RG80G-45717)

OPPOSITE BOTTOM: Supplies are carried above the cliff along the same path taken by some of the Rangers during their assault on Pointe du Hoc on D-Day, June 6, 1944. Here, aerial bombardment and naval gunfire has brought down a portion of the cliff face. While shortening the distance that the Rangers had to rope up the vertical cliff face, the exposed wet clay that composed this ledge was a menace to forward progress. (National Archives, RG80G-45718)

OPPOSITE: A Ranger's eye view of the cliff face. A toggle rope, a tubular ladder, and a further two ropes are all suspended from above the cliff at this point. One might imagine how exposed the Rangers must have been to German small arms fire and grenades during their climbs, making the feat all the more remarkable. (National Archives, RG80G-45716)

ABOVE: After having been evacuated from the fighting in Normandy by an LCVP, wounded Rangers and German prisoners are brought aboard the battleship U.S.S. *Texas* stationed offshore of Pointe du Hoc, June 7, 1944. (National Archives, RG80G-235586)

ABOVE: In a photo released on June 12, 1944, 2nd Battalion Rangers rest momentarily amid the destruction on Pointe du Hoc, France, after seizing this position from the Germans on the morning of D-Day, June 6, 1944. The Ranger seated at right appears to be working the grit out of a magazine for his M1 carbine. (National Archives, RG80G-45715)

OPPOSITE: A sailor helps a wounded Ranger officer to the sick bay aboard the U.S.S. *Texas*. A vertical white bar, nicknamed an 'aiming stake', was applied to the back of the helmet to denote officers; NCOs were denoted by a horizontal white bar. Over these were painted the orange lozenge with the number 2 or 5 that the Rangers wore on the backs of their helmets for Operation OVERLORD. (National Archives, RG80G-352821)

BELOW LEFT: View of M1 steel helmet with Captain's rank insignia painted on the front. (Courtesy Pete Bennethum)

BELOW: Rear view of same M1 helmet showing the officers' 'aiming stake' vertical white bar and orange lozenge designating 2nd Ranger Infantry Battalion as worn during the D-Day landings. (Courtesy Pete Bennethum)

OPPOSITE BOTTOM: 2nd Rangers gather at Colonel Rudder's temporary command post at Pointe du Hoc on D+2, to rest and consume rations. Pictured side by side with the Rangers here are Sergeant Leonard Goodgal of the 101st Airborne Division (fourth from right), and Lieutenant Colonel Thomas Trevor of the British Commandos (lower right). Goodgal was among a handful of paratroopers who landed in the vicinity of Pointe du Hoc, and who fought alongside the Rangers. Trevor had been assigned to the Rangers as an advisor during their training in England. He landed with them at the Pointe and was creased in the head by a German bullet while crossing the shingle. Undaunted, Trevor strode back and forth along the beach, shouting encouragement to the Rangers, and angry curses at the Germans. (National Archives, RG80G-45721)

Preparing to leave the point on D+2. The relief accomplished by elements of the U.S. 29th Infantry Division, 2nd Rangers joined in drive toward Grandcamp. Colonel Rudder (arrow) had been wounded three times, but accompanied his force. Staff Sergeant Jack Kuhn, is standing at left without helmet and cradling an M1 Thompson submachine gun. (U.S. Army Military History Institute)

ABOVE: Men of 2nd and 5th Rangers at a religious service held in a Norman hedgerow field by the chaplain of the Ranger Force. (U.S. Army Military History Institute)

BELOW: Astride captured horses, two Rangers, Corporal Joseph Sanford (left) of Paterson, New Jersey, and Private William Sisson of Somerville, Massachusetts, report to Captain Edward Luther of Boston, Massachusetts, on their successful mission. All are members of the U.S. 5th Ranger Infantry Battalion. On horseback – 5th Rangers captured some fifty horses from a German artillery unit during the early fighting in Normandy – they conducted a patrol into the French countryside and returned with 53 German prisoners. (National Archives, RG208-AA-24P-2)

ABOVE: After fighting for three days and nights to secure the Allied beachhead in Normandy, the 2nd and 5th Ranger Battalions paused briefly to be resupplied with rations and ammunition, and to reorganize, then were ordered to move into a bivouac near Osmansville, approximately eight miles from Grandcamp, France. While there, the presence of an undetermined number of Germans sheltering in the nearby countryside was reported by a French farmer. A Ranger patrol was dispatched to round up the enemy, who turned out to be a German headquarters unit eager to become prisoners. Pictured from left to right are 5th Rangers, Private Lionel F. Pye, Private Robert Marks (partially hidden behind Pye), Staff Sergeant William E. Boyd, Corporal George Watkins (on bicycle), Captain Robert J. Presatti, and Technician 5th Grade Sherman Goldstein. (National Archives, RG208-AA-24P-1)

BELOW: On D+6, personnel of the 2nd Ranger Battalion rest in the company of their mascot, appropriately named 'Ranger'. One of the Rangers at this communications post samples a bottle of *Saint Emilion* donated by French peasants in the area. (National Archives, RG111-SC-190161)

ABOVE: Officers and men of the 2nd and 5th Ranger Battalions are awarded the Distinguished Service Cross for extraordinary heroism during the invasion of Normandy. The original caption accompanying this picture lists ten names, however only eight Rangers are pictured. Standing on the far left is Lieutenant Colonel Max F. Schneider, commanding officer of the 5th Ranger Battalion; he has previously been misidentified as Colonel James E. Rudder by an error in the original caption, although Rudder, too, was awarded the DSC for his actions on D-Day. Other DSC recipients, some of them pictured here, are Major Richard P. Sullivan (5th), Captain Otto Masny (2nd), Captain Edgar L. Arnold (2nd), Captain Ralph E. Goranson (2nd), First Lieutenant Joseph R. Lacy (5th), Second Lieutenant George F. Kerchner (2nd), Technical Sergeant John W. White (2nd), Sergeant Julius W. Belcher (2nd), and Private First Class William E. Dreher, Jr. (2nd). Other recipients from the 2nd Ranger Battalion not pictured include, Sergeant William J. Courtney, First Sergeant Leonard G. Lomell, First Lieutenant William D. Moody, and Private First Class Otto K. Stevens. (National Archives, RG111-SC-190997)

Preparing a message to be radioed back to the 5th Ranger Battalion command post are, left to right, Technician 4th Grade Norman C. Seeley, Private First Class Louis Biava, and Private Henry P. Piekarz, near Brest, France, August 17.

ABOVE: OD herringbone twill jacket as worn by 2nd and 5th Battalion Rangers during the D-Day landings and the campaign in Normandy. (Courtesy Joe Ranoia)

ABOVE LEFT: OD herringbone twill trousers and M1938 dismounted leggings worn by a member of the U.S. 5th Ranger Battalion during the battle for France, 1944. (Courtesy Joe Ranoia)

LEFT: OD wool flannel shirt worn by a member of the U.S. 5th Ranger Infantry Battalion. The 'Ranger' lozenge shoulder sleeve insignia is hand-made, presumably in France, and is of the earliest design worn by that battalion. The Combat Infantryman's Badge is cloth embroidered. (Courtesy Joe Ranoia)

FAR LEFT: Gold bullion shoulder sleeve insignia of the 5th Ranger Battalion. (Courtesy Joe Ranoia)

RIGHT: Hand made insignia worn by a member of the 83rd Chemical Mortar Battalion which air assaulted southern France by glider as part of the 1st Airborne Task Force in August 1944. (Courtesy Dr. Mort Cohen)

Major General Robert T. Frederick, commanding officer of the 1st Airborne Task Force, an ad hoc unit of parachute and gliderborne units cobbled together in Italy for the airborne assault of south France, receives the town flag from the citizens of Le Muy, France, after American forces liberated the town, 17 August 1944. Previously, Frederick was the commander of the famed Canadian-American First Special Service Force, and is regarded by many as being among the most savvy American field commanders of the war. (National Archives, RG111-SC-192771)

Near the Franco-Italian Border, November 1944. Crew of the half-track, dubbed *Ace of Spades*, pounds a distant enemy target with indirect fire from their 'French 75'. While at Anzio, Italy, the First Special Service Force inherited Darby's Ranger Force's Cannon Company, consisting of four M3 gun motor carriages mounting M1897A 75mm field guns. (United States Military History Institute)

November 29, 1944, issue of Yank Magazine featuring on the cover members of the First Special Service Force preparing for combat in Southern France near the Franco-Italian Border. Private Barney Snyder (right) helps Technician 4th Grade Harry Owens load on his pack before setting out with a field-modified .30" Browning M1919A4 light machine gun. Snyder, called the 'Daniel Boone of the Maritime Alps' by his buddies, carries extra rifle grenades in the pockets of his mountain trousers. The Nazis called the men of the FSSF 'Black Devils' after the fighting along the Mussolini Canal at Anzio. (Author's Collection)

ABOVE: The Office of Strategic Services was, by Presidential military order, born on June 13, 1942. Its director was General William J. ('Wild Bill') Donovan. The OSS answered directly to the Joint Chiefs of Staff, and during the war performed three major functions: to conduct intelligence gathering activities; to assimilate "raw" information and transmit items of "finished intelligence" to proper civilian and military end users; and to carry out paramilitary operations in coordination with conventional Allied military operations. The paramilitary branch of OSS was further divided into two distinct sections: Jedburgh, and Operational Groups. Pictured is an American Jedburgh readying his equipment prior to being inserted into France by parachute. (National Archives, RG226-FPL-T-78)

RIGHT: Padded camouflage cloth insertion helmet of British design as worn by OSS agents for clandestine parachute drops. (Courtesy Hayes Otoupalik)

Camouflage insertion suit of British Government manufacture as sometimes used by U.S. Jedburgh team members. (Courtesy Hayes Otoupalik)

By 1944, the Office of Strategic Services was participating in Operation JEDBURGH, a coordinated effort between the United States, Great Britain, and the Free French. The Jedburgh mission was to assist in the training, arming, and equipping of resistance forces in enemy-occupied countries, and to liaison with resistance leaders in order to assure that Allied plans were being carried out. Each Jedburgh consisted of a three-man team: one American OSS officer or one British officer from a similar agency (typically SOE), one Free French officer, and an enlisted radio operator. Individual team members were most often referred to as Jeds. Each Jed wore the military uniform of his home country so that in the event of capture, he stood less chance of being executed as a spy. Here, a Jedburgh team gets dressed for a mission. The American team member, foreground left, wears a reinforced M1942 jump suit, and is armed with an M1911A1 automatic pistol and an unmarked Fairbairn-Sykes style stiletto. (National Archives, RG226-FPL-T-172)

INSET: Unmarked OSS Fairbairn-Sykes style stiletto and sheath with 'pancake flipper' belt frog. (Courtesy Hayes Otoupalik)

SPECIAL RECON BN
SPECIAL RECON. BN.
VICTOR J GIANINNO
01304060 T42 A
CATHERINE GIANINNO
906 PEARL ST
ELKHART IND C
A 5
Burma 101 Campaign
OSS

OPPOSITE: Captain Victor J. Gianinno grouping including two variations of the OSS Special Reconnaissance Battalion scroll, China-Burma-India shoulder patch, 5307th Composite Unit patch, U.S. Fifth Army patch, OSS Detachment 101 pin, button compass, escape pencil, 'Stinger' zip gun, identification tag, Silver Star medal, service ribbons, 'Donavan's Devils' pin, 'OSS' pin that was available to OSS veterans in the fall of 1945, cloth parachutist's roundel, and U.S. parachutist's wings. (Courtesy Hayes Otoupalik)

RIGHT: OSS Hamilton Aero button compass of Captain Victor J. Gianinno. (Courtesy Hayes Otoupalik)

BELOW: OSS escape pencil of Captain Victor J. Gianinno. The metal spike with attached string was concealed inside of a hollow in this pencil. (Courtesy Hayes Otoupalik)

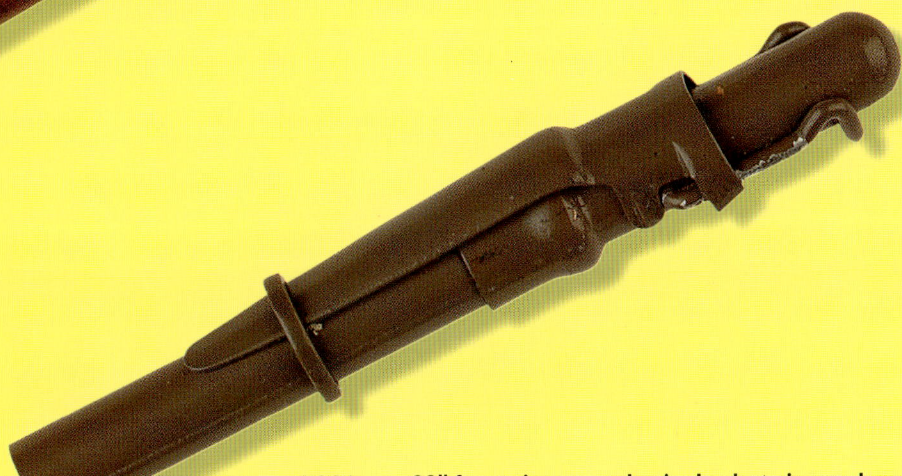

OSS issue .22" fountain pen-style, single-shot zip-gun known as the 'Stinger'. (Courtesy Hayes Otoupalik)

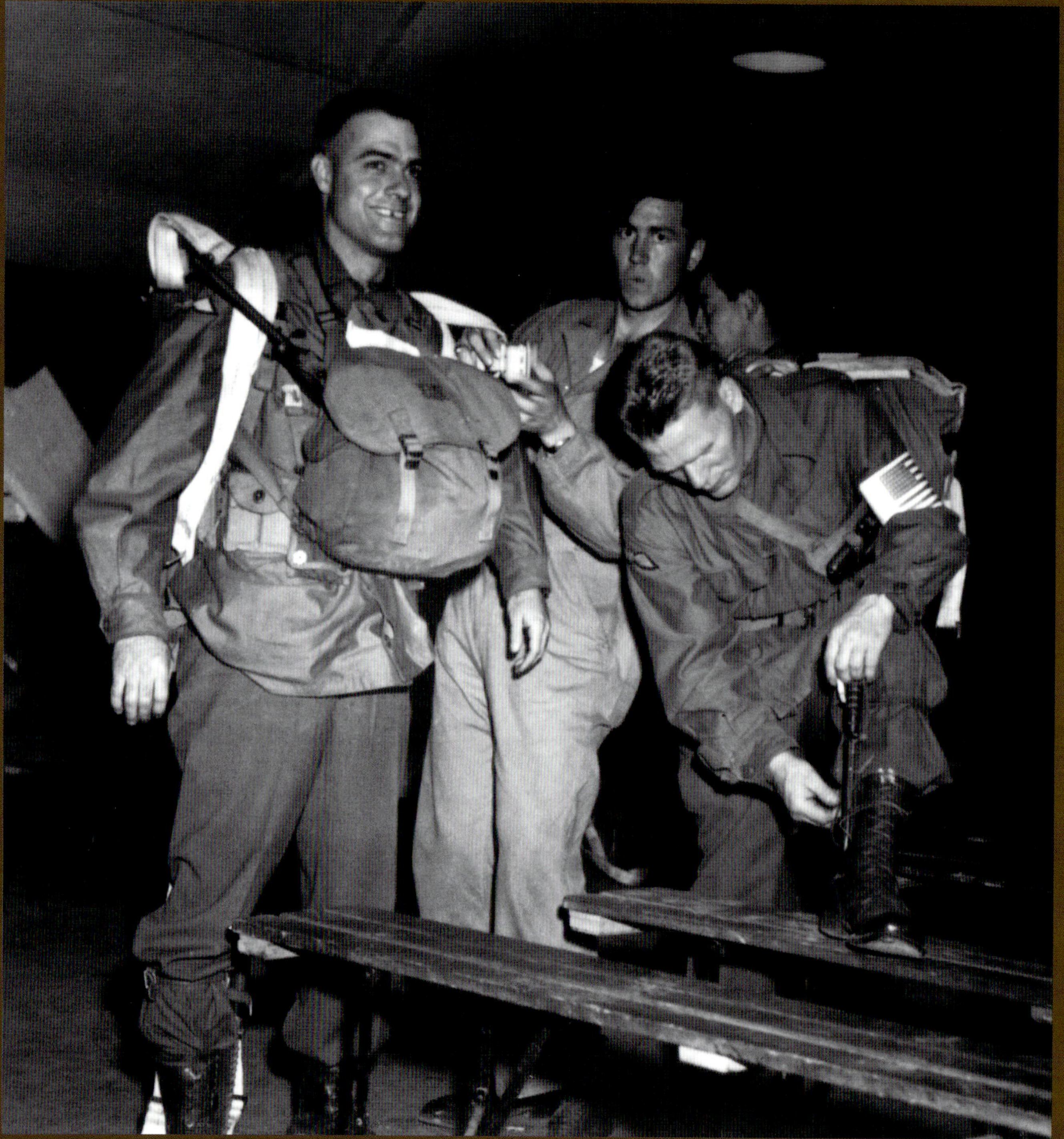

A pair of hearty looking OGs are helped on with their parachutes, Harrington Airdrome, England, c. 1944. OSS Operational Groups, an exclusively American venture, consisted of as few as 15 operatives to more than 30, depending on mission requirements. While the role of Operational Groups was essentially the same as that of the Jedburghs, the OGs' capability for offensive action was measurably more robust. Often working in coordination with Jedburgh teams and local underground forces, OGs led forays against enemy troops and installations, gathered intelligence, and conducted counterscorch operations. Like their Jedburgh counterparts, OGs were uniformed troops. The men chosen for duty in the OSS possessed bravery, ingenuity, and personal initiative. Those who passed initial screening were sent on to more highly intensive training that would prepare them for the rigors that lay ahead. To Scottish training camps like Arisaig, recruits came to be trained by experts in subversive warfare. In his book, *The O.S.S. and I*, William J. Morgan states that the training consisted of "demolitions, map-reading, compass-work, rapid firing, silent killing, fieldcraft, rope-work, tumbling, living off the land, and a few para-naval tactics. The students had to climb hand over hand up precipitous cliffs, swing off high ledges by ropes tied to trees, shoot at moving targets while running over bogs, sand, or rocks, toss live grenades and shoot tracer bullets, hold an advanced post in an empty house against 'enemy' fire and deal with an ambush on a lonely road." The training problems were most realistic, acclimating the pupils to what they might have to tackle on actual missions. (National Archives, RG226-FPL-T-152)

Chester James Bartz Grouping. Chester Bartz (at right in the inset photograph) was born July 25, 1922, in Chicago, Illinois. He was inducted into federal service, Army of the United States, on February 25, 1943, in Chicago. He went on active duty beginning on March 4, 1943. Bartz's military occupation specialty (#746) was as an Automatic Rifleman. During the course of his World War II service, Bartz earned the Combat Infantryman Badge, and the U.S. Parachutist Badge (Parachute Jumping School, Geoia, Italy, September 12, 1944), the Good Conduct Medal, the American Theater Service Ribbon, the European-African-Middle Eastern Service Ribbon with one bronze 'invasion' Arrowhead, and the Asiatic-Pacific Service Ribbon (and the World War II Victory Ribbon).

Bartz participated in numerous campaigns including Rome-Arno, Northern Apennines, Central Europe, and China Offensive. As part of the Central Europe campaign, Bartz trained Yugoslav partisans in explosive demolitions and raiding and night fighting techniques and led them on a number of raids throughout the Dalmatian Islands against German forces. In total, Bartz spent 1 year, 5 months, and 20 days in service overseas. His date of separation is November 3, 1945.

In Bartz's own words, he, "served with the 2671st Special Reconnaissance Battalion in the European Theater of Operations. Loaded, aimed and fired an automatic rifle in combat with [the] enemy. Fired either automatic or in short bursts as directed. [Have] knowledge of all infantry hand weapons. Awarded three battle stars. Was in China for six months training Chinese troops in the use of infantry weapons and tactics. OSS OG helped form first Chinese Paratroopers. Trained Chinese troops in the use of infantry weapons and tactics. Formed Chinese Commandos. All American troops helped to form branches of Chinese Commandos. I was attached to 1st Branch, 8th Commandos."

Of special interest in the grouping are the U.S. flag brassard, the small Yugoslavian national banner, and the enameled insignia of the Chinese Commandos. (Courtesy Hayes Otoupalik)

RIGHT: Black spray paint camouflaged M43 field jacket, worn and faded by actual field use. This example was found with no shoulder sleeve insignia. However, the imprint of the 'Special Recon Bn' scroll that once adorned this jacket is clearly evident. The scroll pictured was added for the sake of this photograph. The 2671st Special Reconnaissance Battalion was organized into companies, each charged with operations in different parts of the Mediterranean. A Company, Italian Operations; B Company, French Operations; and C Company, Balkan Operations. Late in the war, B and C Companies were transferred to the CBI. (Courtesy Hayes Otoupalik)

LEFT: An OSS 2671st Special Reconnaissance Battalion scroll insignia belonging to OG Chester J. Bartz. (Courtesy Hayes Otoupalik)

LEFT: Wool service coat of Technician 5th Grade Chester J. Bartz of the OSS' 2671st Special Reconnaissance Battalion. Both the U.S. Seventh Army shoulder sleeve insignia, and the Special Reconnaissance Battalion scroll are hand-made and of Italian origin. (Courtesy Hayes Otoupalik)

RIGHT: 2nd Pattern Fairbairn-Sykes knife carried by OSS OG Technician 5th Grade Chester J. Bartz. (Courtesy Hayes Otoupalik)

A stout NORSO OG is helped on with his British X-type parachute in the dressing hut at Area T, Harrington Airdrome, Northern England, c. 1944. During July 1943, while the ethnic-Norwegian 99th Infantry Battalion (Separate) was training at Camp Hale, Colorado, it was visited by representatives from the OSS who asked for volunteers. Interviews with Norwegian Army and OSS officers followed. Among other things, the candidates learned that they must agree to parachute training. Of those who offered themselves, eighty enlisted men and twelve officers were selected. This group was transferred to Washington, DC, where the men were organized into a unit of Norwegian Operational Groups, code named NORSO, intended to lead a guerrilla war against the German forces in Norway in advance of a proposed large-scale Allied operation. (National Archives, RG226-FPL-T-168)

RIGHT: M1C steel helmet, designed for use by parachute troops, with M1944 net cover and elastic foliage band. (Courtesy Kirk B. Ross)

NORSO OGs listen to an RAF briefing officer prior to boarding aircraft at Harrington Airdrome, for a mission in France, c. 1944. In schools and training areas in the Mid-Atlantic and in New England, the NORSO operators began their OSS initiation with courses in small boat handling, in demolitions, and in small arms. Movement overseas in December 1943, brought NORSO to a new training area near Swansea, Wales, for practical field work and physical toughening. Parachute training for NORSO members was held at the British Airborne Forces training school at Ringway Airdrome, Manchester, England. After five parachute jumps, the last from a hot air balloon, the OSS men received the British parachute qualification badge. The use of legbags was also a part of parachute training. These large canvas bags, which could be filled with all manner of ammunition, explosives, rations, and personal effects, were attached to the jumper's leg before exiting the aircraft, and then detached while in descent and lowered on a fifteen foot line before reaching the ground. Once finished at Ringway, NORSO went to Scotland to complete its training. Yet, when NORSO was ready for a mission in Norway, Norway was not ready for them. (National Archives, RG226-FPL-T-145)

Members of an OSS OG stand under the wing of an all-black B-24 at Harrington Airdrome, Buckinghamshire, England, that will deliver them to France, c. 1944. By spring of 1944, Anglo-American intentions centered on France, and the opening of a second front in Normandy. For the time being there could be no sweeping Allied operation in Norway. Furthermore, a uniformed OG operation in Norway might only serve to excite the Norwegian resistance into a premature uprising, inviting its annihilation at the hands of the vengeful Germans. But, rather than keep NORSO inactive, it was decided to employ its OGs in France, in support of the Allied invasion. As the time grew nearer to launching the cross-Channel attack, Operation OVERLORD, resistance and intelligence gathering missions within occupied France grew in frequency and in intensity. Primary road and railroad arteries, some as far away as Southern France, increasingly became targets for sabotage with an eye toward hampering the movement of German reinforcements and supplies to the Calvados Coast of Normandy. Between June and September 1944, from bases in England, and Algeria, as many as ninety Jedburgh teams were parachuted into France. During that same time period, a total of twenty-two Operational Groups – four being NORSO OGs – also entered France, parachuting far inland. (National Archives, RG226-FPL-T-96)

LEFT: Detail of hand-made embroidered parachutist's cloth oval, and OSS 2671st Special Reconnaissance Battalion scroll belonging to Captain Victor J. Gianinno. Beginning in 1944, the OSS organized its OGs operating in the Mediterranean area under the 2671st designation. (Courtesy Hayes Otoupalik)

BELOW: Detail of embroidered British parachutist's qualification badge as awarded to OSS personnel who completed parachute training under a British-sponsored system. This example belonged to OSS OG Technician 5th Grade Chester J. Bartz. (Courtesy Hayes Otoupalik)

US
U.S.
U.S.

OPPOSITE: Lieutenant Colonel Prince Serge Obolensky (at center with hands on hips) stands with a number of his OGs and his briefing officer prior to setting off from Area T, for a mission in France, c. late June 1944. By winter 1944-1945, the necessity for resistance activity within France began to wane as the Allied armies pressed north and east into Belgium and Holland, and toward the German frontier. During their so-called 'second march through France', it is estimated that the contribution of the *Forces Françaises de l'Intérieur*, or *Maquis* as they were sometimes called, to the Allied cause was equal to that of fifteen divisions. This feat was, to some extent, made possible by the training, weapons, leadership, and other support provided to the *Maquis* by the courageous Jedburghs and OSS Operational Groups. During its operations in France, NORSO was commanded by Lieutenant Colonel Obolensky. During World War I, Obolensky served as a Czarist Russian cavalry officer. In the wake of the 1917 Bolshevik Revolution, Obolensky made his way to the United States where he became a successful stockbroker. After the outbreak of World War II, Obolensky, at age forty-nine, joined the U.S. Army as a private. He was immediately recruited into the OSS and promoted to Major. The Operational Group concept is credited to Obolensky. With the OSS, Obolensky led a number of successful missions, and helped train the NORSO group whose men idolized him. (National Archives, RG226-FPL-T-165)

INSET: British pattern parachute jumper's knee pads as worn by OSS OGs. (Author's Collection)

ABOVE: Their mission completed, a Jedburgh trio now awaits reassignment, vic. Macon, Southern France, September 9, 1944. At left, U.S. Navy Seaman 3rd Class, Gerard Litalien – who made five parachute jumps for the U.S. Army – jumped into France in May for the Office of Strategic Services to work with the *Forces Françaises de l'Intérieur* prior to the invasion. Lieutenant Jean Marin, center, of Carolles, France, commissioned by the London office, is in civilian clothes. Canadian Army Captain L. Guy D'Artois, right, of Montreal, Canada, formerly with the First Special Service Force, also arrived in France via parachute in May 1944, sent by the OSS to organize the *Maquis* and distribute American and British weapons dropped by planes. The battle of Bois Clair, according to one version, involved five-hundred FFI men against fifteen-hundred Nazis. Results, according to this source, were over five-hundred German casualties, while the FFI lost but twelve killed. (National Archives, RG111-SC-235941)

Major General William B. Kean, presents Private First Class Carl Berg of the 99th Infantry Battalion (Separate), the Silver Star and a promotion to Sergeant, for gallantry in action, Belgium, December 1, 1944. The 99th Battalion (Separate), arrived in Great Britain on September 17, 1943. In England, and in Whales, the battalion conducted unarmed combat and 'Ranger' training. On June 25, 1944, the battalion landed in France, across Omaha Beach, scene of fierce D-Day fighting. Under the 4th Port Headquarters, the 99th helped to secure the port of Cherbourg, and was then attached to the Provisional Ranger Group through July 24. The battalion captured Elbeuf, France, on August 25, 1944, and later entered Belgium, with the U.S. First Army. On October 16, the 99th Battalion carried out a successful operation to cut the Aachen-Cologne highway at Worselen, Germany. During the Battle of the Bulge, the 99th was rushed to the defense of Malmedy, Belgium, arriving on December 17, 1944. Relieved one month later, the battalion was moved to Barneville, France, on the Normandy coast where it became one battalion of the 474th Infantry Regiment (Separate), joining former Rangers and paratroops of the First Special Service Force. After training and refitting, the 474th entered Germany on April 2, 1945, and then fanned out in the wake of the advancing Third Army to comb the countryside, villages and towns, for enemy war materiel, stragglers, and Nazi guerrillas. Germany surrendered unconditionally on May 8, 1945, and days later the 474th was alerted for movement to Norway. Arriving in Oslo, on June 5, the 474th, as part of a larger task force, assisted in the disarming and repatriation of the nearly 400,000 German troops stranded in Norway at war's end. (National Archives, RG111-SC-431714)

INSET: Examples of shoulder sleeve insignia worn by the 99th Infantry Battalion (Separate). At top, the U.S. First Army insignia was most often worn by the 'Norwegian Avengers' on both field and service uniforms prior to the battalion's deployment to Norway. The middle example is an imprinted cloth insignia made in Norway. The bottom example is the official 99th Infantry Battalion (Separate) shoulder sleeve insignia and is of U.S. manufacture. (Author's Collection)

Tired and haggard, four 5th Ranger Battalion officers look at a copy of the *Stars and Stripes* after returning from fighting on the Third Army front, attached to the U.S. 6th Cavalry Group (Mechanized) near St. Avold, France, December 6, 1944. (National Archives, RG111-SC-367998)

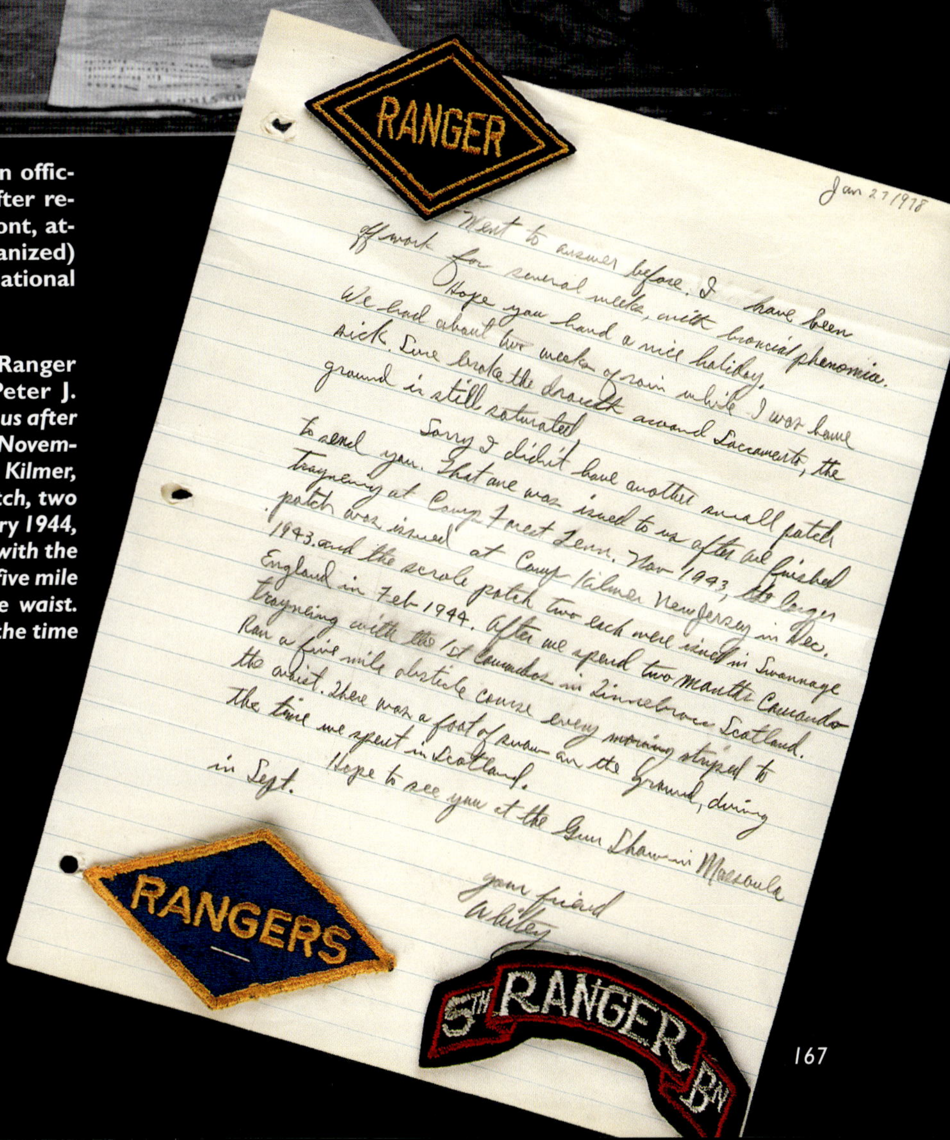

Jan 27 1978

Meant to answer before. I have been off work for several weeks, with broncial phenomia.

Hope you hand a nice holiday. We had about two weeks of rain while I was home sick. Sure broke the draught around Sacramento, the ground is still saturated.

Sorry I didn't have another small patch to send you. That one was issued to us after we finished trayneing at Camp Forest Tenn. Nov 1943, the larger patch was issued at Camp Kilmer New Jersey in Dec. 1943. and the scrole patch two each were issued in Swannage England in Feb 1944. After we spend two months Commando trayneing with the 1st Commandos in Tinselbrouch Scotland. Ran a five mile obstacle course every morning stripped to the waist. There was a foot of snow on the ground during the time we spent in Scotland.

Hope to see you at the Gun Show in Massoula in Sept.

your friend
Whitey

RIGHT: R.M. ('Whitey') Weatherford, 5th Ranger Battalion, letter and patches. (Courtesy Peter J. Bonner): *Excerpt:" small patch ... was issued to us after we finished training at Camp Forest, Tennessee, November 1943. The larger patch was issued at Camp Kilmer, New Jersey, December 1943. And the scroll patch, two each, were issued in Swannage, England, in February 1944, after we spent two months commando training with the 1st Commandos in Tignabruich, Scotland. Ran a five mile obstacle course every morning stripped to the waist. There was a foot of snow on the ground during the time we spent in Scotland."*

ABOVE: In a ceremony held on January 3, 1945, Major General Edwin P. Parker, Jr., commanding officer of the U.S. 78th Infantry Division, congratulates Lieutenant Edward S. Kucinski of the 2nd Ranger Battalion after awarding him the Distinguished Service Cross for extraordinary heroism in combat. (National Archives, RG111-SC-438409)

RIGHT: Action on March 3, 1945, near Heimbach, Germany, shows the 2nd Platoon, C Company, U.S. 2nd Ranger Infantry Battalion, moving cautiously forward along a dirt road through a desolate forest. (National Archives, RG111-SC-341763)

RIGHT INSET: Two examples of U.S. 2nd Ranger Infantry Battalion scrolls. (Courtesy Kirk B. Ross)

LEFT: Homemade 'knuckle' knife carried by a U.S. Ranger in northwest Europe during World War II. Interestingly, the leather sheath has been stitched together with wire 'thread'. (Courtesy Hayes Otoupalik).

Near Rhurburg, Germany, March 3, 1945, in the U.S. First Army zone, men of the 2nd Ranger Battalion's C Company assemble in preparation for movement to the front. (National Archives, RG111-SC-341762)

NORSO members in Oslo, Norway, at war's end. From left to right, Borge Langeland, Kai Johnsen, Major William E. Colby, and Technical Sergeant Matti Raivio, 16 June 1945. The NORSO OGs were withdrawn from France in December 1944, and sent back to Scotland for ski and mountain training. Obolensky, due to his age, retired from military service, and Major William E. Colby took over. In January 1945, the unit was pared down to some fifty operatives. Two months' time would find a number of these men fighting in Norway. By 1945, the German military was in a state of near collapse, but was still a dangerous foe. To within the Fatherland, the remnants of the German Army were converging for what was to be the final battle of the war in Europe. NORSO's mission would be to contain nearly 150,000 German troops presently in northern Norway, so as to prevent their use in the final defense of Germany. That mission, Operation RYPE, was, according to Major Colby, the U.S. Army's first and only ski-parachute operation undertaken during World War II. Winter snows made Norway's roads and highways impassable to motor traffic. Allied naval and air patrols blocked the sea and sky lanes. Operation RYPE – the destruction of the Nordland Railway north of Trondheim – would deny the Germans the use of this last avenue for evacuation from Norway. RYPE commenced on March 24, 1945, when twenty-one OSS operatives, with demolitions, signal, and necessary winter equipment, entered Norway by parachute. On April 15, 1945, NORSO obliterated the Tangen railroad bridge thus severing the Nordland line. David had slain Goliath. A job well done, Colby's group, nevertheless, stayed in Norway, dodging German patrols until the end of the war. (National Archives, RG111-SC-335404)

ABOVE: Service coat and overseas cap belonging to Captain Roger Hall, OSS NORSO Operational Group. Hall wrote about his wartime experiences in, *Your Stepping On My Cloak and Dagger*.

RIGHT: Captain Roger Hall's cloth embroidered Special Forces Airborne wings and his British parachute qualification wings, stitched to the right shoulder sleeve of his service coat. There appear to have been produced three wartime variations of the cloth embroidered 'SF' wings, and also one being bullion embroidered. (Courtesy Peter J. Bonner)

ABOVE: Three piece telescoping flexible metal truncheon belonging to OSS Captain Roger Hall. (Courtesy Peter J. Bonner)

PART IV

Operations in the Pacific and the Far East

In a scene depicting a unit not typically associated with combat in the Asiatic-Pacific Theater of Operations, a 16-man combat section of the joint Canadian-American First Special Service Force rests by the water of the Bering Sea, at Quisling Cove, Kiska, Aleutian Islands, August 15, 1943. Elements of the FSSF spearheaded the invasion to retake the island from the Japanese who had occupied Kiska, since June 6, 1942. Most of the Forcemen are armed with M1 rifles and M1942 bayonets except for the section leader, a Staff Sergeant, armed with an M1A1 submachine gun; all are armed with M1911A1 automatic pistols. They wear M2 helmets with net covers, M1941 arctic field jackets, mountain trousers, and parachute boots. (National Archives, RG208-AA-7E-8)

ABOVE: Woven shoulder sleeve insignia of the 158th Infantry Regiment, Separate, with 'Bushmaster' scroll. These private purchase insignia may have been produced in Australia. (Courtesy Peter J. Bonner)

Men of the 158th Infantry Regiment (Separate), nicknamed 'Bushmasters' after the deadly pit viper of Central America, prowl the uncivilized trails of Panama, near Fort Clayton, Panama Canal Zone, June 13, 1942. The 158th Infantry was inducted into federal service on September 16, 1940, as one regiment of the U.S. 45th Infantry Division. Subsequently relieved from assignment to the 45th Division, the 158th transferred to Panama where it spent all of 1942, in jungle warfare training in the difficult tropical forests of the region. (National Archives, RG111-SC-136146)

Bushmasters construct a 'Wiki-Up' in the dense rainy forests of Panama, c. June 1942. The men of the 158th Infantry stated that the climatic conditions faced during the arduous training in Panama were far worse than any they experienced under actual combat in New Britain, New Guinea, or the Philippines, where the 158th served as a spearhead for attacking U.S. forces. (National Archives, RG111-SC-145752)

Cuidado ("Take Care") distinctive insignia of the 158th In-

RIGHT: Two variations of shoulder sleeve insignia of the 158th Regimental Combat Team embroidered on blue felt. The concept for the 'Regimental Combat Team' was developed by General MacArthur's Southwest Pacific Command to meet the challenge of engaging limited numbers of enemy troops within the confines of small islands or similarly isolated terrain. In essence, the combat team was a flexible, self-sufficient organization made up of combat arms supported by attached service and administrative adjuncts. The 158th Infantry Regiment 'Bushmasters' were the nucleus around which was built the 158th RCT. Other mainstay elements of this RCT included the 147th Field Artillery Battalion, the 506th Medical Collecting Company, and the 1st Platoon, 637th Medical Clearing Company. (Courtesy Peter J. Bonner)

BELOW: A front line position manned by Bushmasters of the 2nd Battalion, 158th Infantry Regiment (Separate), on Arawe, New Britain, January 2, 1944. The troops pictured here are all of Native American extraction. The 158th was an Arizona National Guard organization, and in its ranks as many as twenty Native American tribes were represented. Less well known than those of the United States Marine Corps, but as effective, were the Native American language code talkers of the 158th. (National Archives, RG111-SC-288135)

ABOVE: Bushmaster Private First Class Wallace Grant, a Pima Indian of Laveen, Arizona, lies on the ground after running a message from a patrol to his platoon command post. Private Stephen Lopez, a Papago Indian of Sello, Arizona, phones the message to the company command post. Both men are of F Company, 2nd Battalion, 158th Infantry Regiment on Arawe, New Britain, January 26, 1944. (National Archives, RG111-SC-288140)

OPPOSITE TOP: The smoke of battle hangs heavy in the air as Bushmasters of the 158th Infantry Regiment move forward on Noemfoor Island after debauching from the amphibious tractors that brought them ashore, July 2, 1944. Said General Douglas MacArthur of the 158th Regimental Combat Team, "No greater fighting combat team has ever deployed for battle." (National Archives, RG111-SC-272259)

OPPOSITE BOTTOM: Command post of A Company, 1st Battalion, 158th Infantry Regiment on the far side of Kimiri Airstrip, Noemfoor, July 2, 1944. The Bushmasters, part of the CYCLONE Task Force, landed on the island to capture the airstrip. The field radio being used is carried in a camouflage M1943 jungle pack, improvised to serve as a waterproof cover. (National Archives, RG111-SC-272260)

Two examples of the shoulder sleeve insignia of the 147th Field Artillery Battalion of the 158th Regimental Combat Team. (Courtesy Peter J. Bonner)

OPPOSITE TOP: In the hills near Damortis, Luzon, Philippine Islands, a wounded Bushmaster of the 158th Infantry lies on a litter awaiting evacuation to an aid station in the rear. The Bushmasters entered combat in the Philippines, on January 11, 1945, and remained in the Philippines until war's end. The Bushmasters were then sent to Japan for occupation duty and there inactivated on January 17, 1946. (National Archives, RG111-SC-265274)

BELOW: Group shot of the officers graduating from the third class held at the ASTC (Alamo Scouts Training Center), Finschhafen, New Guinea, June 22, 1944. The Alamo Scouts were born on November 28, 1943, as the U.S. Sixth Army Special Reconnaissance Unit. The mission of the Alamo Scouts was to carry out tactical reconnaissance and intelligence gathering activities in the Pacific area. Attempts by the director of the OSS, William J. Donovan, to establish regular OSS operations in the Southwest Pacific Area were rejected by General Douglas A. MacArthur who preferred instead to create his own intelligence and reconnaissance machinery. (National Archives, RG111-SC-258743)

ABOVE: After hurling a grenade into the building, an Alamo Scouts trainee sprays bullets into this mock Japanese headquarters with his Thompson submachine gun, at the Alamo Scouts Training Center on Fergusson Island, New Guinea, January 17, 1944. Eight Alamo Scouts training classes were held at six separate locations between December 1943, and September 1945. Established first on Fergusson Island, then relocating successively to Finschhafen, Hollandia, Leyte, and finally Luzon, keeping pace with the advance of the U.S. Sixth Army's advance across the Pacific, the ASTC graduated a total of nineteen six-man Alamo Scouts teams. (National Archives, RG111-SC-287236)

INSET ABOVE: Alamo Scouts shoulder sleeve insignia. (Courtesy Peter J. Bonner)

OPPOSITE TOP: Major General J.P. Swift, commanding officer of the U.S. 1st Cavalry Division, watches a combat swimming demonstration as an ASTC instructor fires a .45" submachine gun into the water around Alamo Scouts trainees who must dive to avoid the fire, Fergusson Island, New Guinea, January 17, 1944. During the course of the war the Alamo Scouts carried out over one hundred successful missions, included two prison camp liberations, one at Cape Oransbari, Dutch New Guinea, and the other at Cabanatuan, Luzon, Philippine Islands. Throughout all, no Scout was killed or captured. (National Archives, RG111-SC-287239)

OPPOSITE BOTTOM: Major General Fred H. Osborn, War Department Director of Morale Services, talks with Alamo Scouts following a demonstration of combat swimming with full equipment, ASTC, Fergusson Island, January 11, 1944. (National Archives, RG111-SC-255792)

A party of Alamo Scouts is landed onto the rocky shore of Kwokeboh Island in Tanahmerah Bay, Dutch New Guinea, 1944. To be successful, Alamo Scouts became proficient in a variety of skills including rubber boat handling, intelligence gathering, scouting and patrolling, navigation, survival, communications, and weapons. Scouts traveled light and were armed primarily for self defense. Popular weapons were the M1A1 carbine and the .45" submachine gun. (MacArthur Memorial, SWPA-SC-44-1276)

OPPOSITE TOP: Men and pack mules of the 5307th Composite Unit, Provisional, on the move into the Burma front via the Ledo Road, February 1944. From October 1943, until February 1944, the 5307th, nicknamed 'Merrill's Marauders' by Time-Life writer James Shepley, received an intensive dose of jungle warfare and deep penetration tactics. The march from Ledo to their jumping off point at Shingbwiyang, Burma covered nearly 140 miles. (National Archives, RG111-SC-350136)

OPPOSITE BOTTOM: Their eyes scanning to the front and sides of the jungle trail along which they move, a Marauder patrol serves as vanguard to the 5307th Composite Unit's main body. (National Archives, RG208-MO-6P)

ABOVE: Near Walawbum, Burma, c. March 2-9, 1944, a Marauder checks the body of a dead Japanese soldier for material which might prove valuable for intelligence purposes. In sharp contrast to U.S. Army regulations, Japanese soldiers in the field were permitted to carry all manner of identifying items on their person, such as photographs and diaries. (National Archives, NWDNS-LUBIN-QMM-109)

OPPOSITE: Column of men and pack animals crossing the Tanai Kai River in northern Burma on their way to entering the village of Ningi Awng, March 18, 1944. These men are part of the U.S. 5307th Composite Unit, Provisional, code named GALAHAD. The bridge was built by native Kachin tribesmen who aligned themselves with Allied forces in Burma. (National Archives, RG111 SC 277385)

ABOVE: Marauders Gately (left front) and LaBrun (right front) of Orange Combat Team's Intelligence and Reconnaissance Platoon, 5307th Composite Unit, Provisional, meet some Chinese allies relieving their positions, so that the Marauders may proceed with preparations for their next mission. Northern Burma, March-May 1944. (National Archives, NWDNS-LUBIN-OMM-134)

Portrait photograph of Brigadier General Frank D. Merrill, commanding officer of the 5307th Composite Unit, Provisional. (National Archives, RG111-SC-C2473) INSET: Embroidered (top) and imprinted versions of the China-Burma-India Theatre of Operations shoulder sleeve insignia. (Courtesy Kirk B. Ross)

ABOVE: General Merrill explains the current battle situation to Herb Miyazaki, left, and Akiji Yoshimura, right, interpreters for the 5307th's 3rd Battalion, Hsamshingyang, Burma, c. April 1944. (National Archives, NWDNS-LUBIN-QMM-140)

BELOW: Major Edward Briggs, the 5307th Composite Unit's Khaki Combat Team commander and his staff hold full field inspection at Hsamshingyang, Burma, on April 19, 1944, prior to the commencement of the Myitkyina campaign. (National Archives, RG111-SC-277391)

ABOVE: North of Sitapur, Burma, on the outskirts of Myitkyina, men of E Company, 2nd Battalion, Merrill's Marauders, await the order to resume the attack. (National Archives, RG111-SC-274337)

RIGHT: Embroidered shoulder sleeve insignia of the 5307th Composite Unit, Provisional. (Courtesy Peter J. Bonner)

ABOVE LEFT: Bullion Merrill's Marauders shoulder sleeve insignia. It is likely that this example was locally produced in India. (Courtesy Peter J. Bonner)

BELOW: On the eve of Myitkyina's fall, a group of Marauders sits less than 75 yards from enemy positions, taking time out to read old magazines. August 2, 1944. (National Archives, RG111-SC-350139)

ABOVE: OGs of OSS Detachment 101 at Camp Richie, Akyab, Burma, preparing to head for the nearby beach prior to undertaking a reconnaissance mission to Cheduba Island, January 1945. Like its OSS Operational Group counterparts in Europe and the Mediterranean, Detachment 101 was tasked with infiltrating teams of agents behind enemy lines in order to organize guerrilla warfare units. (National Archives, RG226-FPK-45-27)

OPPOSITE: OSS Detachment 101 operational group at Camp Richie, Akyab, western Burma, with seven-man LCR (landing craft, rubber) readying for departure on a reconnaissance mission to Cheduba Island, off the west coast of the Burmese mainland, c. January 1945. (National Archives, RG226-FPK-45-29)

ABOVE: An American officer of OSS Detachment 101 and a group of Kachin Rangers refer to a map while deep behind Japanese lines near Man Sak, Burma, January 4, 1945, The Kachin Rangers were recruited by the OSS from the Kachin hill people native to north-central Burma in the area through which passed the Ledo Road. The Kachin Rangers participated in the assault on Ramree Island, Burma, on January 27, 1945, and Rangoon, Burma, on May 2, 1945. In between these two battles the OSS-led Kachins participated in numerous other actions. (National Archives, RG111-SC-316727)

RIGHT: OD wool flannel shirt of Technician 4th Grade Chester J. Bartz as worn during the six months he spent in China with the OSS training Chinese volunteers as paratroops and commandos. The scroll of the 2671st Special Reconnaissance Battalion is worn above a hand-made bullion embroidered shoulder sleeve insignia of the China-Burma-India Theatre of Operations. (Courtesy Hayes Otoupalik)

INSET ABOVE: Shoulder sleeve insignia of the OSS sponsored Free Thai. The OSS recruited volunteers from among ethnic Thai university students, both in the United States and in England, and, after their training, inserted them into Thailand to organize and train guerrilla forces to fight the Japanese invaders. (Courtesy Peter J. Bonner)

ABOVE: At Man Sak, Burma, January 4, 1945, Kachin Rangers are dug in in a position overlooking a trail that might come under use by Japanese forces escaping from nearby Namkha. These men are armed with a mix of British Number 4 rifles, and U.S. M3 submachine guns. (National Archives, RG111-SC-330589)

RIGHT: At the U.S. training grounds at Myitkyina, Burma, January 18, 1945, showing a so-called Gorkha Ranger – one of a 390-man detachment of native Kachin tribesmen trained and equipped by the Office of Strategic Services – on duty by the sign post that is just at the edge of their area. During the drive to Myitkyina, Kachin guerrillas served as a screening force and as an intelligence gathering instrument for Merrill's 5307th Composite Unit, Provisional. Now their main duty is to guard the entire area of Myitkyina. (National Archives, RG111-SC-257231)

OPPOSITE: OSS Detachment 404 Maritime Unit swimmers wearing the U.S. Lambertsen diving jacket (left), and a British-designed respiratory apparatus. The Lambertsen unit was used for both long underwater swims and in conjunction with the Mark VI submersible canoe. The British unit was for use with the canoe only. (National Archives, RG226-FPK-SEAC-45-184)

ABOVE: Sergeant Edward Arida of New York City, OSS Detachment 101, is receiving a message from other OSS agents reporting from behind enemy lines in northern Burma, January 27, 1945. At his side are three Kachin Rangers, assigned to the U.S. 124th Cavalry Regiment, an element of the 5332nd Brigade, Provisional, also known as the MARS Task Force. While Arida operates the radio set, one of the Kachins cranks the hand-powered generator. (National Archives, RG111-SC-316736)

BELOW: Standing on the beach at Galle, Ceylon, May 1, 1945, Captain Lillyman, a British instructor, explains the mechanisms of the various underwater respiratory apparatus to OSS Detachment 404 Maritime Unit personnel. Detachment 404 operated another field station at Kandy, Ceylon, as well. (National Archives, RG226-FPK-SEAC-45-186)

X-7

ABOVE: View of the one-man Mark VI submersible canoe, nicknamed the 'Sleeping Beauty', Galle, Ceylon, May 1, 1945. The principal headquarters for OSS Detachment 404 was at Kandy, Ceylon. Established in November 1943, Detachment 404 was responsible for overseeing operations in Thailand, Malaya, Sumatra, and the parts of Burma not covered by Detachment 101. (National Archives, RG226-FPK-SEAC-45-187)

BELOW: Captain Lambertsen pilots the Mark VI to the surface, Galle, Ceylon, May 1, 1945. The OSS Maritime Unit was tasked with planning covert infiltration operations by sea, landing agents by sea, conducting resupply operations to resistance groups by sea, carrying out maritime sabotage, and with further development of related equipment. (National Archives, RG226-FPK-SEAC-45-196)

ABOVE: Major Robert W. Garrett (foreground), executive officer of the U.S. 6th Ranger Infantry Battalion, stands before other headquarters group officers at Base 'F', Finschhafen, New Guinea, October 9, 1944. The 6th Ranger Battalion was activated at Hollandia, New Guinea on September 24, 1944, with personnel from the 98th Field Artillery Battalion, and other volunteers. The 6th Ranger Battalion was organized along the same lines at their European counterparts, and was commanded by Lieutenant Colonel Henry A. Mucci. (National Archives, RG111-SC-292567)

ABOVE INSET: U.S. 6th Ranger Battalion shoulder sleeve insignia. (Courtesy Peter J. Bonner)

ABOVE: Major Robert Garrett inspects men of B Company, 6th Rangers, at Base F staging area, Finschhafen, New Guinea, October 1944. These Rangers are attired in OD herringbone twill jackets and trousers. They use U.S. Marine Corps style camouflage cotton twill helmet covers with elastic or rubber foliage bands. Note that Major Garrett has taped over the metal rank insignia on his right collar. (National Archives, RG111-SC-261058)

RIGHT: Camouflage cotton twill helmet cover as used by the U.S. 6th Ranger Infantry Battalion. (Courtesy Hayes Otoupalik)

BELOW: Men of E Company, 6th Ranger Battalion, climb down the net scramble of an assault personnel destroyer onto the deck of a waiting LCPR (landing craft, personnel, ramp), lying offshore of Leyte Gulf, Philippines, October 17, 1944. Their objective is Dinagat Island, one of three islands at the entrance to Leyte Gulf; the capture of which will be the prelude to U.S. Sixth Army's invasion of Leyte. These Rangers all wear B3 life preserver vests. (National Archives, RG111-SC-255841)

A Ranger's view of Dinagat's smoke shrouded Black Beach, from the inside of an LCPR carrying elements of the 6th Ranger Battalion ashore in the first wave, October 17, 1944. The mission of the Rangers during this operation was to capture Dinagat, Homonhon, and Suluan Islands astride the channel leading into Leyte Gulf. Dinagat and Homonhon were secured with little opposition; the Rangers then installed beacons on these two islands to guide the invasion fleet through the channel between them. (National Archives, RG111-SC-255839)

OPPOSITE: A patrol of F Company, 6th Ranger Battalion, investigates native huts on Dinagat Island, Philippines, October 17, 1944. On neighboring Suluan Island, B Company Rangers, after a daring climb, surprised and destroyed a Japanese outpost ensconced in and around the island's lighthouse perched atop an imposing cliff. (National Archives, RG111-SC-255842)

LEFT: Similar to their Ranger counterparts in the Mediterranean and Northwest Europe, the 6th Ranger Battalion utilized LCPRs for beach landings. In this photograph, U.S. Navy personnel stand by a beached LCPR that was used to land elements of the 6th Rangers on Dinagat Island, offering an excellent view of the bow ramp over which the Rangers exited the boat. (National Archives, RG111-SC-255843)

255842

ABOVE: Shortly after the U.S. Sixth Army invaded Luzon, Philippines, on January 9, 1945, it learned of a Japanese prison camp near Cabanatuan, holding a large number of American PWs. On January 27, 1945, preceded by three Alamo Scouts teams and Filipino Guerrillas, 107 Rangers of C and E Companies, 6th Ranger Battalion, cross a shallow river as they begin a twenty-four mile trek behind enemy lines to liberate the camp. Speed and stealth were of prime importance, so helmets and heavier equipment were left behind. (National Archives, RG111-SC-201177)

RIGHT: C and E Companies, 6th Ranger Battalion advance through a sea of grass near San Rosario, Luzon, on their way to rescue some 500 Americans, prisoners of the Japanese being held at a camp eight miles east of Cabanatuan City, Philippines, January 27, 1945. (National Archives, RG111-SC-396872)

RIGHT: Fighting knife manufactured for U.S. 6th Ranger Battalion personnel in the Philippines. During the war, the image of this knife was incorporated into the unofficial insignia of the 6th Rangers. (Courtesy Hayes Otoupalik)

BELOW: These Filipino Guerrillas are among those who guided the U.S. 6th Rangers on their mission to free American prisoners being held by the Japanese near Cabanatuan. After thorough reconnaissance by the Alamo Scouts, the Rangers commenced their attack on the camp on the evening of January 30. In the sharp battle that ensued, the Rangers killed more than 200 of the enemy at a cost of two dead. As the Rangers and freed Americans withdrew, the Filipino Guerrillas remained behind as a blocking force, thwarting a Japanese relief column. (National Archives, RG111-SC-201178)

OPPOSITE TOP: Private First Class Roy Bruno, a Browning automatic rifleman of C Company, 6th Rangers, talks shop with guerrilla Private Eulogio, also a BAR gunner, at the evacuation hospital, Guimba, Luzon, Philippines, January 31, 1945, following the successful mission to free American PWs from the Japanese. (National Archives, RG111-SC-377702)

OPPOSITE BOTTOM: U.S. 6th Rangers discuss their successful Cabanatuan prison raid. One of the recently freed Americans, wearing shorts, stands behind the group. (National Archives, RG111-SC-387162)

377702

Mission accomplished. 6th Ranger Private First Class Vernon M. Abbott carries Technical Sergeant Charles G. Mortimer, an injured ex-prisoner of war released from the prison camp near Cabanatuan, Luzon, Philippines, into the evacuation hospital at Guimba, Luzon, January 31, 1945. (National Archives, RG111-SC-201655)

RANGER RESOURCES
A SELECT BIBLIOGRAPHY

Altieri, James J., *Darby's Rangers: An Illustrated Portrayal of the Original Rangers, World War II, In Training and In Action*, (Arnold, Missouri, Ranger Book Committee, 1977).

Altieri, James J., *The Spearheaders*, (New York, Bobbs-Merrill, 1960).

Arnbal, Anders Kjar., *The Barrel-Land Dance Hall Rangers: World War II, June 1942-February 1944*, (New York, Vantage, 1993).

Arthur, Anthony, *Bushmasters: America's Jungle Warriors of World War II*, (St. Martin's Press, New York, 1987).

Black, Robert W., *Rangers In World War II*, (Ballantine Books, New York, 1992).

Burhans, Lt. Col. Robert D., *The First Special Service Force, A War History of the North Americans 1942-1944*, (Infantry Journal Press, Inc., Washington, 1947).

Darby, William O., and Baumer, William H., *We Led the Way: Darby's Rangers*, (New York: Berkley, 1985).

Ewing, Joseph H., *29th Let's Go!*, (Infantry Journal Press, Inc., Washington, 1948).

Gabbett, Michael, The Bastards of Burma: *Merrill's Marauders and the Mars Task Force Revisited*, (Desert Dreams Publishers, Albuquerque, 1989).

Hall, Roger, *You're Stepping On My Cloak and Dagger*, (W.W. Norton & Company, Inc., New York, 1957).

Hogan, Jr., David W., *Raiders or Elite Infantry?: The Changing Role of the U.S. Army Rangers from Dieppe to Grenada*, (Greenwood Press, Westport, Connecticut, 1992).

Hogan, Jr., David W., *U.S. Army Special Operations in World War II*, (Center of Military History, Washington, 1992).

Hopkins, James E.T., with Jones, John M., *Spearhead: A Complete History of Merrill's Marauder Rangers*, (Galahad Press, Baltimore, 1999).

Ingersoll, Ralph M., *The Battle Is the Payoff*, Fighting Forces Series (Washington, DC: Infantry Journal Press, 1943).

Ladd, James D., *Commandos & Rangers of World War II*, (St. Martin's Press, Inc., New York, 1978).

Lane, Ronald L., *Rudder's Rangers*, (Manassas, Virginia: Ranger Associates, 1979).

Morgan, William J., *The O.S.S. and I*, (W.W. Norton & Company, Inc., New York, 1957).

Ogburn, Jr., Charlton, *The Marauders*, (Harper & Brothers Publishers, New York 1959).

Ross, Robert T., *The Supercommandos: First Special Service Force 1942-1944, An Illustrated History*, (Schiffer Publishing, Ltd., Atglen, Pennsylvania, 2000).

Smith, Bradley F., *The Shadow Warriors: O.S.S. and the Origins of the C.I.A.*, (Basic Books, Inc., New York, 1983).

Stanton, Shelby L., *World War II Order of Battle*, (Galahad Books, New York, 1991).

U.S. Army, 99th Infantry Battalion, *History of the 99th Infantry Battalion, U.S. Army*, written by PFC Howard R. Bergen, (Oslo, Norway: Emil Moestue. 1946).

U.S. War Department, Historical Division, "France: 2d Ranger Battalion at Pointe du Hoe." *Small Unit Actions*, (Historical Division, War Department, Washington, DC, 1946, pp. 4-56).

Wiriyawit, Wimon, Free Thai: *Personal Recollections and Official Documents*, (White Lotus Press, Bangkok, 1997).

Zedric, Lance Q., *Silent Warriors of World War II: The Alamo Scouts Behind Japanese Lines*, (Pathfinder Publishing of California, Ventura, 1995).

Further Ranger and Special Operations historical information for this book was obtained through the National Archives and Records Administration, College Park, Maryland, as well as through numerous United States Army libraries, including that of the United States Army Military History Institute, Carlisle Barracks, Pennsylvania, the Infantry School, Fort Benning, Georgia, and the Special Operations Command, Fort Bragg, North Carolina.

AMERICAN FLIGHT JACKETS: A History of U.S. Flyers' Jackets from World War II to Desert Storm, Second Edition. *Jon A. Maguire & John P. Conway.* This comprehensive look at the evolution of the American flight jacket from World War I to Desert Storm and addresses not only the types worn, but focuses primarily on the art and adornment applied to the jackets. The most colorful and creative period for flight jacket art was WW II, and it is this era that comprises a major portion of this book. Also covered are other military jackets used by flyers. This revised second edition includes a new section of jackets and period photos.
Size: 9" x 12" • over 1000 color and b/w photographs • 280 pp.
ISBN: 0-7643-1065-8 • hard cover • $69.95

ART OF THE FLIGHT JACKET: Classic Leather Jackets of World War II. *Jon A. Maguire & John P. Conway.* Following the success of their first volume American Flight Jackets, Airmen & Aircraft: A History of U.S. Flyers' Jackets from World War I to Desert Storm, Jon Maguire and John Conway focus solely on the painted leather jackets of the World War II years in this all new volume.
Size: 8 1/2" x 11" • over 600 color and b/w photos • 176 pp.
ISBN: 0-88740-794-3 • hard cover • $49.95

MORE SILVER WINGS, PINKS & GREENS: An Expanded Study of USAS, USAAC, & USAAF Uniforms, Wings & Insignia • 1913-1945 (Including Civilian Auxiliaries). *Jon A. Maguire.* All new material that greatly expands on the items presented in the first book. Additionally, this work covers totally new areas including Civil Air Patrol, W.A.S.P.s, Air Transport Command, Factory Techincal Representatives, and "Yanks" in the RAF and RCAF. Also included are uniforms and insignia of the First World War era, and the "Golden Age" of the 1920s-1930s. There is also a large section on Aviation Cadets and civilian contract flying schools and instructors. Includes period photographs showing the items as they were worn.
Size: 8 1/2" x 11" • over 1,100 color and b/w photos • 350 pp.
ISBN: 0-7643-0091-1 • hard cover • $79.95

LUFTWAFFE vs. RAF: Flying Clothing of the Air War, 1939-45. *Mick J. Prodger.* An up-close and serious examination of the various patterns of flight jackets, suits, headgear and gloves worn by the courageous pilots and aircrews of these two great adversaries during WWII. This book includes a look at some of the more bizarre and experimental outfits as well as the standard flying kit for different climates and regions, with a special section on electrically-heated clothing. Also examined is the parallel development of flying clothing in the Luftwaffe and the Royal Air Force, and the surprising influence each country had upon the other.
Size: 9" x 12" • over 500 color and b/w photographs • 160 pp.
ISBN: 0-7643-0234-5 • hard cover • $49.95

LUFTWAFFE vs. RAF: Flying Equipment of the Air War, 1939-45. *Mick J. Prodger.* This volume closely examines the development and uses of personal flying equipment of the Luftwaffe and RAF throughout WWII. Compasses secreted in tunic buttons, floating rations, and even suits with built-in parachutes. All types of parachutes and harnesses, life preservers, inflatable boats, survival tools, weapons for self-defense, and even some of the paperwork and personal items carried by the airmen. Study the sophisticated rescue and survival equipment available to Luftwaffe crews, alongside the clever, yet often brilliantly simple devices which enabled so many RAF flyers to evade capture.
Size: 9" x 12" • over 500 color and b/w photographs • 144 pp.
ISBN: 0-7643-0249-3 • hard cover • $49.95

EAGLES RECALLED: Pilot and Aircrew Wings of Canada, Great Britain and the British Commonwealth 1913-1945. *Warren Carroll.* These pieces of cloth and metal symbolize the daring, bravery, suffering and loss of men who flew in deadly aerial battles for democratic freedom. Much of the material contained in this publication has never been published. The author has also made new historical discoveries presented here for the very first time - he has accessed private collections, photographed rare museum acquisitions, and received support from historians in seven countries over a period of some ten years. This work brings to readers a detailed and comprehensive study of the brevets issued to aviators who fought with Great Britain in World Wars I and II.
Size: 8 1/2" x 11" • over 800 color and b/w photos • 240 pp.
ISBN: 0-7643-0244-2 • hard cover • $79.95

VINTAGE FLYING HELMETS: Aviation Headgear Before The Jet Age. *Mick J. Prodger.* This new book explores the history and development of early flying headgear throughout the pioneering nations in military and sport aviation, from the earliest exploits of the Wright Brothers, to the end of World War II. Drawn from aviation museums and private collections from around the world, the illustrated color section features over 1000 photographs depicting more than 650 different items of flying headgear: helmets, goggles, oxygen masks and accessories, including many unique personalizations and rarely seen items.
Size: 9" x 12" • over 1,000 color and b/w photographs • 336 pp.
ISBN: 0-88740-776-5 • hard cover • $75.00

JET AGE FLIGHT HELMETS: Aviation Headgear in the Modern Age. *Alan R. Wise & Michael S. Breuninger.* This is the first book ever to cover in detail the history and development of military flight helmets from the post-World War II era to the present, and includes over 120 different helmets and their associated equipment such as oxygen masks, boom microphones, inner helmets etc. Specific details of each helmet include manufacturer, proper designation, unique features, accessories, periods of use, branch of service(s), and aircraft in which is was used-selected export users are also included. Mike Breuninger is also the author of
Size: 9" x 12" • over 1,000 color and b/w photographs • 248 pp.
ISBN: 0-7643-0070-9 • hard cover • $75.00

PILOTS' INFORMATION FILE 1944: The Authentic World War II Guidebook for Pilots and Flight Engineers. The Pilots' Information File (PIF) was the standard reference for any general information required of USAAF pilots and flight engineers. The PIF covered items of a general nature that a combat flyer must know in order to fight an air war and survive.
Size: 8 1/2" x 11" • photographs, drawings, diagrams • 268 pp.
ISBN: 0-88740-780-3 • soft cover • $19.95

THE M-1 HELMET: A History of the U.S. M-1 Helmet in World War II. *Mark A. Reynosa.* Presents over seven years of research into the history of the M-1 helmet during World War II, and provides the most comprehensive examination of its development and production. All aspects of M-1 helmet production are covered including: the helmet body, the fiber liner, the plastic liner, the parachutist helmet, helmet camouflage, helmet modifications, helmet paint schemes, and toy helmets. Every production helmet version is presented in full color photographs, including detail shots and production markings. Also included are World War II era photographs of the helmet samples, helmet production, and helmets worn in training or in action. This book is a valuable reference to both historians and collectors.
Size: 8 1/2" x 11" • over 350 color and b/w photos • 112 pp.
ISBN: 0-7643-0074-1 • hard cover • $39.95

POST-WORLD WAR II M-1 HELMETS: An Illustrated Study. *Mark A. Reynosa.* This book presents several years of research into the history of America's post-World War II M-1 Helmet. It provides the most comprehensive look into the research, development, and production of the M-1 Helmet during this often overlooked period. All aspects of the M-1 Helmet are covered, as well as associated research and development programs that impacted the helmet, such as the Nylon Helmet Program. Included are contract sheets, contract number reference, military specification drawings, and photos of helmet samples and production.
Size: 8 1/2" x 11" • over 260 color and b/w photos • 136 pp.
ISBN: 0-7643-1033-X • hard cover • $39.95